Books by Joyce Carol Oates

JOYCE CAROL OATES

THE EDGE OF
IMPOSSIBILITY:

---

tragic forms in
literature

The Vanguard Press, Inc., New York

Library of Congress Catalogue Card Number: 77–188692
SBN 8149–0675–3
Manufactured in the United States of America
Designer: Ernst Reichl

for Evelyn Shrifte

I dream that I am told: "The revelation, the answer to all your questions can only come to you in a dream. You must have a dream." So, in my dream, I fall asleep and I dream, in my dream, that I'm having the absolute dream. On waking, that's to say on really waking, I remember having dreamed that I'd dreamed, but I can remember nothing about the dream within a dream, the dream of absolute truth, the dream that explained everything.

I am so very true that I cannot escape from myself. I organize myself. I am the self that organizes myself thus, arranging the same materials in a unique pattern.

Ionesco, Fragments of a Journal

ACKNOWLEDGMENTS "The Tragedy of Existence: Shakespeare's *Troilus and Cressida*," is drawn from two essays, one of which appeared in *Philological Quarterly*, Spring 1967, and the other of which appeared in *Shakespeare Quarterly*, Spring 1966. "The Tragedy of Imagination: Shakespeare's *Antony and Cleopatra*," appeared in *Bucknell Review*, Spring 1964; "Melville and the Tragedy of Nihilism" appeared in *Texas Studies in Literature and Language*, Spring 1962; "Tragic and Comic Visions in *The Brothers Karamazov*" appeared in *The Journal of Aesthetics and Art Criticism*, Winter 1968–69; "Chekhov and the Theater of the Absurd" appeared in *Bucknell Review*, Winter 1966; "Art at the Edge of Impossibility: Mann's *Dr. Faustus*" appeared in *The Southern Review*, Spring 1969; "Ionesco's Dances of Death" appeared in *Thought*, Fall 1965; "Yeats: Violence, Tragedy, Mutability," appeared in *Bucknell Review*, Winter 1969–70; "Tragic Rites in Yeats' *A Full Moon in March*" appeared in *The Antioch Review*, Winter 1969–70.

CONTENTS

INTRODUCTION:
Forms of Tragic
Literature

We seek the absolute dream. We are forced back continually to an acquiescence in all that is hallucinatory and wasteful, to a rejection of all norms and gods and dreams of "tragedy" followed by the violent loss of self that signals the start of artistic effort: an appropriation by destruction, or an assimilation into the self of a reality that cannot be named. The art of tragedy grows out of a break between self and community, a sense of isolation. At its base is fear. If it is not always true that human life possesses value, it is at least true that some human life, or the abstract parody of human life as acted out by gods, has a profound and magical value, inexplicable. The drama

3

begins only when a unique human reality asserts its passion against the totality of passion, "arranging the same materials in a unique pattern," risking loss of self in an attempt to realize self—there steps forward out of the world an Oedipus, an Antigone. The making of domestic landscapes into wilderness is the aspect of tragedy that always shocks us, for in our wholesome terror we cannot conceive of the justification of our lives calling forth a death of passion, an annihilation of passion—what are we except passion, and how are we to survive when this passion breaks its dikes and flows out into nature?

The hero at the center of tragedy exists so that we may witness, in his destruction, the reversal of our private lives. We adjust ourselves to the spectacle of an art form, we paralyze our skepticism in order to see beyond the artifice of print or stage, and we share in a mysterious dream the necessary loss of self, even as this self reads or watches, losing ourselves in the witnessing of someone's death so that, in our human world, this hero may be reborn. The tragic hero dies but is reborn eternally in our dreams; the crudity of our desire for an absolute— an absolute dream, an absolute key—is redeemed by the beauty that so often surrounds this dream. One can explain the dream but never its beauty.

The hero dies into our imaginations as we, helplessly, live out lives that are never works of art—even the helpless lives of "artists"!—and are never understood. Suffering is articulated in tragic literature, and so this literature is irresistible, a therapy of the soul. We witness in art the reversal of our commonplace loss of passion, our steady loss of consciousness that is never beautiful but only biological. Therefore our love for art, and our resentment of it. We consume ourselves into a present without horizon, and without value; the creations of our imagination consume themselves into a marvelous future, a universal future in which we somehow share. The object of our fascination, in Husserl's words, *gives itself as having been there before reflection,* and we feel that the triumph over nothingness that art represents is assured of a future beyond even our ability to imagine. We acclaim the marvelous in ourselves.

Of the many contemporary critics who have written on tragedy, George Steiner and Lionel Abel are among the most provocative. Steiner's thesis, like that of Joseph Wood Krutch before him, is that tragedy is dead. We have heard this often, we will be hearing it often: "Tragedy is that form of art which requires the intolerable burden of God's presence. It is dead now because His shadow no longer falls upon us as it fell upon Agamemnon or Macbeth or Athalie." If it returns it will be in a new form, and Steiner implies that it will be a form perhaps unintelligible to the West. In his brief, strange book, *Metatheater,* Abel tries to solve the critical problem of the relationship between "tragedy" and less pure forms of drama by denying that tragedy is a natural Western art form at all. According to Abel, Shakespeare wrote no tragedies, with the possible exception of *Macbeth.* The dominant dramatic form is not tragedy but "metatheater"—the kind of drama that assumes the total subjectivity of the world and its metamorphosis, by way of a mysterious psychological process, into theater. Theater as *theater,* as self-conscious and ironic subjectivity—this is "metatheater."

What are we to make of such assumptions? Does the frequent appearance in dramatic literature of the world-as-stage and life-as-dream bring along with it the actual

5

valuelessness of the contextual world? Where is history? Where is personal history? Certain critics are always convinced that an epoch creates art, but a great work always tells us that it is isolated, unique, accidental, and inexplicable—not even the possession of the creator himself—and that its true context is not history but dreams, ahistorical dreams. Like a personality, a work of art occurs once, and, re-experienced, is redefined; it has no "existence" at all. But to argue backward from this insight, to argue that the dreamlike quality of a work of art indicates a dreamlike, nihilistic culture beyond it, is irresponsible. If Hamlet represents the most developed figure of Western "metatheater," then he is a prince of nihilism and nothing more. According to Abel, "One cannot create tragedy without accepting some implacable values as true. Now, the Western imagination has, on the whole, been liberal and skeptical; it has tended to regard *all* implacable values as false." But from what ground does the play arise? What is its fundamental delusion? If the play is *Hamlet,* the hero's delusion is certainly not that he cannot locate truth, but rather that he cannot reject it powerfully enough; though appearances argue that all values are false, Hamlet's tragedy is that he cannot accept appearances. Out of his faith comes the tragedy.

Nothing can come from nothing, no energy from a bodiless spirit; thus, there can be no violence out of a sense of nothing, for violence is always an affirmation. Abel claims that the West has always been nihilistic in its imaginative literature, but how can such an assumption account for its very shape, the structural consummation of violent action? Art is built around violence, around death; at its base is fear. The absolute dream,

6

if dreamed, must deal with death, and the only way toward death we understand is the way of violence. In the various works examined in this collection of essays, as well as in *Hamlet*, nihilism is overcome by the breaking-down of the dikes between human beings, the flowing forth of passion; Melville alone, with his essentially religious and superstitious imagination, can create a tragedy of "nihilism." In our ingenious theater of the absurd, and to some extent in Chekhov, the dramatic structure itself becomes equated with the sense of loss and inertia of the fictional characters, who are incapable of violence except as victims. And yet they perpetuate acts of violence, by being victims. Here human life is microscopic, imagined as magical and reductive to an instant in time, as in *Waiting for Godot*: "One day we were born, one day we'll die, the same day, the same second. . . . They give birth astride of a grave, the light gleams an instant, then it's night once more." In Beckett we have a true delight in boredom and in the boring of others, a powerful substitute for ancient types of aggression.

Parody is an act of aggression. Twentieth-century literature is never far from parody, sensing itself anticipated, overdone, exhausted. But its power lies in the authenticity of its anger, its parodistic instinct, the kind of art in which Mann's Adrian Leverkühn and Dostoevski's Ivan Karamazov excel: "the playing of forms out of which life has disappeared." If it is true, as George Steiner argues, that the death of God means the death of tragedy, then we need to ask what tragedy has dealt with all along—has it not been the limitations of the human world? What is negotiable, accessible, what can be given proper incantatory names, what is, in Nietzsche's phrasing, "thinkable" —this is the domestic landscape out of which the wilderness will be shaped. If communal belief in God has diminished so that, as writers, we can no longer presume upon it, then a redefinition of God in terms of the furthest reaches of man's hallucinations can provide us with a new basis for tragedy. The abyss will always open for us, though it begins as a pencil mark, the parody of a crack; the shapes of human beasts—centaurs and satyrs and their remarkable companions—will always be returning with nostalgia to our great cities.

1

THE TRAGEDY OF EXISTENCE:

Shakespeare's "Troilus and Cressida"

Troilus and Cressida, that most vexing and ambiguous of Shakespeare's plays, strikes the modern reader as a contemporary document—its investigation of numerous infidelities, its criticism of tragic pretensions, above all, its implicit debate between what is essential in human life and what is only existential are themes of the twentieth century. Philosophically, the play must be one of the earliest expressions of what is now called the "existential" vision; psychologically, it not only represents the puritanical mind in its anguished obsession with the flesh overwhelming the spirit, but it works to justify that vision. It is not only the expense of spirit in a "waste of shame" that is catastrophic, but the expenditure of all spirit—for the object of spiritual adoration (even if, like Helen, it is not unfaithful) can never be equivalent to the purity of energy wasted. Shakespeare shows in this darkest and least satisfying of his tragedies the modern, ironic, nihilistic spectacle of man diminished, not exalted. There is no question of the play's being related to tragedy; calling it one of the "dark comedies" is to distort it seriously. This is tragedy of a special sort—the "tragedy" the basis of which is the impossibility of conventional tragedy.

This special tragedy, then, will be seen to work within the usual framework of tragedy, using the materials and the structure demanded of an orthodox work. What is withheld—and deliberately withheld—is "poetic justice." Elsewhere, Shakespeare destroys both good and evil together, but in *Troilus and Cressida* the "good" characters are destroyed or destroy themselves. The "evil" characters (Achilles, Cressida) drop out of sight; their fates are irrelevant. Ultimately, everyone involved in the Trojan War will die, except Ulysses and Aeneas, and it may be that Shakespeare holds up this knowledge as a kind of backdrop against which the play works itself out, the audience's knowledge contributing toward a higher irony; but this is probably unlikely. The play as it stands denies tragic devastation and elevation. It follows other Shakespearean tragedies in showing the annihilation of appearances by reality, but the "reality" achieved is a nihilistic vision. Thus, Pandarus closes the story by assuming that many in his audience are "brethren and sisters of the holddoor trade" and by promising to bequeath them his "diseases." The customary use of language to restore, with its magical eloquence, the lost humanity of the tragic figure is denied here. Othello is shown to us first as an extraordinary man, then as a man, then as an animal, but finally and most importantly as a man again, just before his death; this is the usual tragic curve, the testing and near-breaking and final restoration of a man. Through language Othello ascends the heights he has earlier relinquished to evil. But in *Troilus and Cressida* Troilus ends with a declaration of hatred for Achilles and a promise to get his revenge upon him. He ends, as he has begun, in a frenzy. His adolescent frenzy of love for Cressida gives way to a cynical, reckless frenzy of hatred for Achilles. Nowhere does he attain the harmonious equilibrium required of the tragic hero or of the man we are to take as a spokesman for ourselves. Even his devastating scene of "recognition" is presented to the audience by a device that suggests comedy: Thersites watching Ulysses watching Troilus watching Cressida with Diomed. Troilus is almost a tragic figure—and it is not an error on Shakespeare's part that he fails to attain this designation, for the very terms of Troilus' experience forbid elevation. He cannot be a tragic figure because his world is not tragic but only pathetic. He cannot transcend the sordid banalities of his world because he is proudly and totally of that world, and where everything is seen in terms of merchandise, diseases, food, cooking, and the "glory" of bloodshed, man's condition is never tragic. That this attitude is "modern" comes as a greater surprise when one considers the strange, fairy-tale background of the play (a centaur fights on the Trojan side, for instance) and the ritualistic games of love and war played in the foreground.

Shakespeare's attempt here to pierce the conventions demanded by a typical audience's will takes its most bitter image in the various expressions of infidelity. Infidelity is the natural law of the play's world, and, by extension, of the greater world: woman's infidelity to man, the body's infidelity to the soul, the infidelity of the ideal to the real, and the larger infidelity of "time," that "great-sized monster of ingratitudes." Here, man is trapped within a temporal, physical world, and his rhetoric, his poetry, even his genius cannot free him. What is so modern about the play is its existential insistence upon the complete inability of man to transcend his fate. Other tragic actors may rise above their predicaments, as if by magic, and equally magical is the promise of a rejuvenation of their sick nations (Lear, Hamlet, etc.), but the actors of *Troilus and Cressida,* varied and human as they are, remain for us italicized against their shabby, illusion-ridden world. Hector, who might have rejected a sordid end, in fact makes up his mind to degrade himself and is then killed like an animal. As soon as he relinquishes the "game" of chivalry, he relinquishes his own right to be treated like a human being, and so his being dragged behind Achilles' horse is a cruel but appropriate fate, considering the violent climate of his world. One mistake and man reverts to the animal, or becomes only flesh to be disposed of. As for the spirit and its expectations— they are demonstrated as hallucinatory. No darker commentary on the predicament of man has ever been written. If tragedy is a critique of humanism from the inside,[1] *Troilus and Cressida* is a tragedy that calls into question the very pretensions of tragedy itself.

In act 2, scene 2, the Trojans have a council of war, and Troilus and Hector debate. What they say is much more important than why they say it, a distinction that is also true about Ulysses' speeches:

14

HECTOR
> Brother, she is not worth what she doth cost
> The holding.

TROILUS
> What is aught but as 'tis valued?

HECTOR
> But value dwells not in particular will;
> It holds his estimate and dignity
> As well wherein 'tis precious of itself
> As in the prizer. (2.2.51–56)

Questions of "worth," "cost," and "value" permeate the play. Human relationships are equated with business arrangements—the consummated love of Troilus and Cressida, for instance, is a "bargain made," with Pandarus as legal witness. Here, it is Helen who is held in question, but clearly she is incidental to this crisis: Hector insists, along with most Western philosophers, that there is an essential value in things or acts that exists prior to their temporal existence and their temporal relationship to a "particular will." They are not created by man but exist independently of him. In other words, men do not determine values themselves, by will or desire or whim. Values exist *a priori*; they are based upon certain natural laws, upon the hierarchy of degree that Ulysses speaks of in the first act. Hector parallels Ulysses in his belief that "degree, priority, and place,/ Insisture, course, proportion, season, form,/ Office, and custom" (1. 3. 86–88) are observed not only by man but by the natural universe. What is strange is that any personal guidance, any evidence of gods or God, is omitted; though the Olympian gods are concerned with the Trojan War, and even though a centaur fights magnificently in the field, the

15

gods ultimately have nothing to do with the fate of the men involved. Like Greek tragedy, this play has certain "vertical" (or universal) moments that coincide with but can sometimes be only weakly explained by their "horizontal" or narrative position. The speeches of Ulysses and Hector are set pieces of this vertical sort, since they explain and insist upon values that must be understood so that the pathos to follow will be more clearly understood; the speeches are always out of proportion and even out of focus, compared to the situations that give rise to them. At these points—significantly, they come early in the play—there is a straining upward, an attempt on the part of the characters to truly transcend their predicaments. The predicaments, however, cannot be transcended because man is locked in the historical and the immediate. Ulysses' brilliance cannot trigger Achilles into action, and, when Achilles wakes to action, all semblance of an ordered universe is destroyed; Hector is destined to kill a man "for his hide" and then to die ignobly, and so his groping after absolute meaning in act 2 must be undercut by a complete turnabout of opinion, when he suddenly and inexplicably gives in to the arguments of Troilus and Paris.

Troilus, the "essentialist" in matters concerning his own love, the weakly romantic courtier who has been transformed simply by the anticipation of love, is in this scene the more worldly and cynical of the two. Though he speaks of the "glory" of the war and Helen as a "theme of honor and renown" who will instigate them to deeds that will "canonize" them, his conviction that man creates all values out of his sense experiences is much more worldly than Hector's Platonic idea that values exist prior to and perhaps independent of experience.[2]

16

Reason itself is called into question: Helenus is accused by Troilus of "furring" his gloves with reason, and reason is equated with fear (2. 2. 32); "Nay, if we talk of reason,/ Let's shut our gates, and sleep." This exchange is usually interpreted as pointing up Troilus' infatuation with honor as an extension of his infatuation with Cressida, but this insistence upon the relativity of all values is much "harder" (to use William James's distinction between "hard" and "soft" thinkers) than Hector's. What is most surprising is that this comes after Troilus' earlier condemnation of Helen (she is "too starved a subject" for his sword). Hector, in his reply, calls upon a supratemporal structure of value that is at all times related to the rather sordid doings of Greeks and Trojans: actions are "precious" in themselves as well as in the "prizer." His argument, based upon the "moral laws of nature" that demand a wife be returned to her husband, parallels Ulysses' prophetic warnings concerning the unleashing of chaos that will result in a son's striking a father dead. Hector says:

> There is a law in each well-order'd nation
> To curb those raging appetites that are
> Most disobedient and refractory. (2.2.180–183)

In doing so, he has shifted his argument from the universal to the particular, speaking now of "law" within a nation and not "law" that exists prior to the establishment of any human community. If this shift, subtle as it is, is appreciated, then Hector's sudden decision a few lines below is not so surprising. He gives so many excellent reasons for wanting to end the war, then says, "Yet, ne'ertheless,/ My spritely brethren, I propend to you/ In resolution to keep Helen still. . . ."

17

No doubt there is something wrong with the scene; no audience would ever be prepared for Hector's sudden change of mind. But it is necessary for the play's philosophic core that the greatest of the Trojans for some inexplicable reason will turn his back on reason itself, aligning himself with those of "distempered blood" though he seems to know much more than they. The scene makes sense if it is interpreted as a demonstration of the ineffectuality of reason as reason, the relativity of all values, and the existential cynicism that values are hallucinatory in the sense that they are products of man's will. As Troilus says, "My will enkindled by mine eyes and ears,/ Two traded pilots 'twixt the dangerous shores/ Of will and judgment" (2. 2. 63–65). Must Troilus be seen as a "lecher," as one critic calls him,[3] because he does not recognize that only marriage is sanctioned by heaven, not courtly love? On the contrary, it seems clear that Shakespeare is pointing toward a criticism of all values in the light of what we know of their origin—through the senses—and that Troilus' flaw is not his inability to understand a moral code, but his humanity.

The limitations and obsessions of humanity define the real tragedy of this play and perhaps of any play, but only in *Troilus and Cressida* does Shakespeare refuse to lift man's spirit above them.[4] And it is certainly no error on the playwright's part that the highly moral, highly chivalric Hector changes into quite another kind of gallant soldier when he is alone. In act 5, scene 6, Hector fights with Achilles and, when Achilles tires, allows him to escape; no more than a minute later he sees another Greek in "sumptuous" armor[5] whom he wants to kill "for his hide." Why the sudden change? It may well be that through allowing Achilles freedom, Hector gains greater glory for himself, and so his "chivalric" gesture is really an egoistic one. (Achilles has said earlier that he is over-confident and a little proud, despite everyone's opinion of him—4. 5. 74–75.) His sudden metamorphosis into a killer can be explained by the relativity of values in even the most stable of men when he can act without witnesses. Though the mysterious Greek runs away and really should not be chased, Hector does chase him and kill him. He does this out of lust for the man's armor; he has refrained from killing Achilles because of his egoistic desire to uphold his reputation. The scene is also an allegorical little piece (most of the scenes involving Hector have an obviously symbolic, "vertical" thrust) that suggests that Death himself is present on the battlefield, tempting everyone with an external show of sumptuousness. Shakespeare, therefore, in two carefully executed though puzzling scenes, shows the upholder of "essentialist" views to switch suddenly and inexplicably to the opposite. His psychological insight is extraordinary here, for though the narrative inconsistency of Hector may baffle an audience, he shows that the will does indeed utilize knowledge for its own sake; "knowledge" may be in control but only because the will at that moment allows it. Jaspers speaks of the desire of man to subordinate himself to an "inconceivable supersensible" and to the "natural character of impulses and passions, to the immediacy of what is now present," [6] and it is this tragic instability of man that Shakespeare demonstrates.

The debate between what is essential and what is existential is carried on in a kind of running battle by Thersites, who speaks as a debased, maddened Fool licensed to roam about the Greek field. An intolerable character, and not at all an amusing one, he speaks with an intelli-

19

gence equal to Ulysses' but without any of Ulysses' control. He is "lost in the labyrinth of [his] fury," and we need not ask what he is so furious about: it is the condition of life itself. He counters Ulysses' speech on degree by various parodies of degree, Ulysses' analytical mind transformed in Thersites into a savage talent for splitting distinctions:

> Agamemnon is a fool to offer to command Achilles;
> Achilles is a fool to be commanded of Agamemnon;
> Thersites is a fool to serve such a fool; and
> Patroclus is a fool positive. (2.3. 67–71)

His curses are a disharmonious music that balances the overly sweet music attending Helen, and the result of his relentless cataloguing is certainly the calling-down of all ideals as they have been expressed in the first two acts of the play:

. . . Here's Agamemnon, an honest fellow enough, and one that loves quails, but he has not so much brain as ear-wax: and the goodly transformation of Jupiter there, his brother, the bull, the primitive statue, and oblique memorial of cuckolds . . . to what form but that he is should wit larded with malice and malice forced with wit turn him to? To an ass, were nothing: he is both ass and ox; to an ox, were nothing: he is both ox and ass. To be a dog, a mule, a cat, a fitchew, a toad, a lizard, an owl, a puttock, or a herring without a roe, I would not care; but to be Menelaus! . . . . (5.1. 56 ff.)

Thersites is to the Greeks and Trojans as the Fool is to Lear, except they learn nothing from him. While Ulysses in his famous speech on "degree" strains to leave the earth and to call into authority the very planets them-

20

selves, Thersites grovels lower and lower, sinking into the earth and dragging with him all the "glory" of this war: "Lechery, lechery! Still wars and lechery! Nothing else holds fashion." He is almost ubiquitous, this maddened and tedious malcontent, and if his cynicism is exaggerated in regard to what he has actually seen, so are the romantic and chivalric ideals of the first half of the play exaggerated in regard to their objects. Thersites runs everywhere, from scene to scene, hating what he sees and yet obviously relishing it, for he is the very spirit of the play itself, a necessary balance to its fraudulent idealism. Significantly, he disappears just when the battle begins in earnest. He is last seen just after Patroclus is reported killed by Hector. After this, the action throws off all ceremonial pretensions, and men go out in the field to destroy, not to play a game. Once Achilles announces that he will kill Hector in "fellest manner," we have no need for Thersites, who is of value only to negate pretensions. Perhaps he does return, in the figure of Pandarus—for the mocking, loathsome Pandarus who ends the play seems a new character altogether. He is really Thersites, but Pandarus is needed to unify the love plot: the play's final word is "diseases," a fitting one certainly, but one that makes more sense in Thersites' mouth than in Pandarus'. Thersites' is the most base, the most existential vision in the play, and if we hesitate to believe that it is also Shakespeare's vision, we must admit that he has spent a great deal of time establishing it. His function is to call everything down to earth and to trample it. In his discordant music he celebrates what Troilus and others have been experiencing, and it is certainly Shakespeare's belief, along with Thersites', that "all the argument is a cuckold and a whore."

21

The play's great theme is infidelity, and it is this that links together the various separate actions. There are three stories here—that of Troilus and Cressida, that of the Greeks' quarrel with Achilles, and that of Hector's downfall—and all three pivot around a revelation or demonstration of infidelity. Casting its shadow over the entire play, of course, is the infidelity of Helen. But it is not even a serious matter, this "fair rape"; it is a subject for bawdy jests for all except Menelaus. "Helen must needs be fair, / When with your blood you daily paint her thus," (1. 1. 95–96) Troilus observes bitterly, but a reflection of this type is little more than incidental. From time to time Greeks and Trojans register consciousness of what they are doing, but in general the games of love and war are enjoyed for their own sakes. It is characteristic of men to give their lives for such activities, Shakespeare suggests, not characteristic of just these men. It is characteristic of all love to be subject to a will that seems to be not our own, and, as Troilus says, "sometimes we are devils to ourselves" (4. 4. 95). Cressida is not just Cressida but all women—the other woman in the play, Helen, is no more than a mirror image of Cressida. When Troilus says that Cressida has depraved their mothers, he is not speaking wildly but speaking symbolically. Hector's sudden about-face is not freakish, but natural; Achilles brutality is not bestial, but human. Above all, the play does not concern isolated human beings but, like all Shakespeare's tragedies, it contains the whole world by implication. Nowhere in the play is it suggested that there is a contrasting life somewhere else. Pandarus' impudent address to the audience is intended to link his pandering with that of the audience's generally, and to suggest that the play is a symbolic piece, the meanings of which accord with the experiences of the audience. This should be understood if the play is to be recognized as a kind of faulty tragedy and not just a farce or satire.

The infidelity theme is illustrated on many levels, some of them ingenious. Shakespeare's conception of his art as existing in a kind of multidimensional sphere—his use, for instance, of structure to comment upon content —is nowhere so brilliant as in this play. It has been noted that *Othello* takes place in a double time,[7] the foreground being the "timeless" time of the tragic narrative that is universal and the background an attempt to set up a plausible chronological order; in *Troilus and Cressida* Shakespeare uses structure to point up his irony, the discrepancy between man's ideals and what he makes of them in reality. It is not "the world" as such that violates man's ideals; it is man himself. The play begins with symmetrically balanced scenes: Troilus and Pandarus, then Cressida and Pandarus; the great Greek council of war, then the Trojan council; the central position (act 3, scene 2) of Paris and Helen, the magnificent lovers and the cause of the war, who are shown to be, unfortunately, insipid and vulgar. We move back and forth from Greek to Trojan worlds, and then, near the end of the play, the two are brought together when Cressida gives herself to the Greek Diomed. After this, the play seems to fall apart. Chaos threatens. The death of Hector is a butchery, and yet Hector has debased himself before his death. Troilus does not kill Diomed or Achilles but simply vows revenge; this is the last we see of him. Pandarus closes the play, not because what would seem to be a normal narrative has ended but because the play's points have been made. Characters act in order to illustrate meanings, and then they disappear; there is no reason even to

23

punish them, for justice is clearly not the way of the world, and certainly the infidelity of Cressida is a "given" for the audience, not a surprise. Here, Shakespeare uses technique to illustrate theme. The almost geometric precision of the play's beginning is matched by the chaos of its ending. Its fairy-tale plots give way to psychological reality, and men live in earnest, thus precipitating the chaos that Othello envisioned as coming when love is destroyed. On a rather abstract level, we have the "infidelity" of the play's unfolding as contrasted with its promises as a seemingly conventional work dealing with a familiar story.

The more literal demonstrations of infidelity deal with the relationship between man and woman, the relationship of man and time, the relationship of man with his ideals, and the relationship of the soul and the body. The most interesting of these is the last-mentioned, because in a sense it includes all the others.

Much, certainly, has been written on the theme of "time" in this play,[8] and Ulysses' marvelous speech calls attention to itself as one of the important set-pieces of the play. But the whole conception of "time" as having supplanted eternity rests upon an existential basis—the mortality of spirit and the corruptibility of the flesh; that is, Ulysses in act 3 rejects philosophically what he has said in the "degree" speech in act 1. It is no matter that all Ulysses is trying to do is to spur Achilles into action—no desire in the play is ever equivalent to the homage paid to it; what is important is the assumption behind each of his lines:

> Time hath, my lord, a wallet at his back,
> Wherein he puts alms for oblivion,
> A great-siz'd monster of ingratitudes:

> Those scraps are good deeds past; which are devour'd
> As fast as they are made, forgot as soon
> As done: . . .
>   . . . . O! let not virtue seek
> Remuneration for the thing it was;
> For beauty, wit,
> High birth, vigour of bone, desert in service,
> Love, friendship, charity, are subjects all
> To envious and calumniating time.
> One touch of nature makes the whole world kin, . . .
>
>   (3.3. 148–175)

"One touch of nature makes the whole world kin": a famous line rarely recognized as the savage indictment of human destiny it is. Here, Ulysses quite deliberately equates "high birth, vigor of bone, desert in service, love, friendship, and charity" as victims of "time"; it is not suggested that any of these outweigh the others simply because they are more spiritual. "Vigor of bone" may be calmly equated with "love," for both are leveled by the passage of physical time: "The present eye praises the present object." Man lives only in the present, a continuously changing present that consumes him and goes on to new flesh. This vision of life is possible only to someone who recognizes nothing beyond man as flesh.

So it is no surprise to Ulysses when Cressida behaves as she does. His language loses its bombastic quality once the Greek council scene in act 1 is over and, as the play continues, becomes direct and objective: "All's done, my lord," he tells Troilus when Cressida has exhibited her unfaithfulness. If the "degree" speech is compared with his later lines, it will seem to be pompous and excessively rhetorical.[9] His vision of chaos is a vision so terrifying that he tries to restrain it through the use of tightly controlled language and imagery; there is the sense in this

25

speech, with its interpretation of the cosmos in terms of man, and, most importantly, in terms of Achilles' disobedience, of something weak and false, something wished for rather than believed. Ulysses leaps from the sight of the "hollow" Grecian tents upon the plain to the "heavens themselves" and tries to relate the two. His threat is that if degree is masked, everything will "include itself in power," power will be overcome by will, will by appetite, and appetite will at last eat itself up, a universal wolf confronted with a universal prey. This is certainly ironic in that Ulysses is concerned specifically with power and that his intelligence is of value only as it directs the power of Achilles. While he seems to be speaking against raw power he is really speaking for it; and the greatest chaos of all is to come when Achilles does indeed go into battle, just as everyone wishes. This famous speech, with its evocation of a marvelous, orderly universe threatened by man's willfulness, is, when examined, hardly more than a sophistic façade of rhetoric intended to bring power, will, and appetite into being. It is directed toward the same ends but is never so honest as the speeches of Troilus and Paris defending Helen. Even if the speech is accepted on its literal level, it is philosophically rejected by Ulysses' later speech. Indeed, the tradition of considering Ulysses the wisest person in the play is suspect; as George Meyer points out, his wisdom has clear limitations.[10] He seems to be an instrument rather than a fully realized person. Like a refined Thersites, he "sees" and "knows" things but he has little to do with what happens.

The infidelity of time is not the primary theme of the play, but is rather an illustration of the results of the tragic duality of man, his division into spirit and flesh. If we are to take Troilus as the moral center of the play, then the initiation into the discrepency between the demands of the soul and those of the body is the central tragic dilemma. His experience is a moving one, and the fact that he is surrounded, in his naiveté, with various types of sexual and moral degeneracy should not undercut his experience. Surely, the play is filled with "derision of folly," and its relationship to the comical satires of Jonson and Marston is carefully detailed by Campbell,[11] but the experience of Troilus is not a satirized experience; it is quite clear that Shakespeare is sympathetic with his hero and expects his audience to share this sympathy.

Let us examine Troilus' education in terms of his commitment to a sensualized Platonism, a mystic adoration of a woman he hardly knows. He begins as a conventional lover who fights "cruel battle" within and who leaps from extremes of sorrow to extremes of mirth because he has become unbalanced by the violence of what he does not seem to know is lust. In the strange love scene of act 3, scene 2, with its poetic heights and its bawdy depths, Troilus is giddy with expectation and his words are confused: does he really mean to say that he desires to "wallow" in the lily beds of Cressida's love, or is this Shakespeare forcing him to reveal himself? The scene immediately follows the "honey sweet" scene in which Pandarus sings an obscene song to Paris and Helen and declares that love is a "generation of vipers"; certainly Troilus' maddened sincerity is pathetic in this circumstance, since we have heard Cressida reveal herself earlier and give the lie to Troilus' opinion of her: "she is stubborn-chaste against all suit" (1. 1. 101). After Pandarus brings them together, Cressida says, "Will you walk in, my lord?" (3. 2. 61). Troilus continues his rhetorical declaration of passion by lamenting the fact that

27

the "monstruosity in love" lies in the will being infinite and the execution confined, and she says a second time in what is surely a blunt undercutting of his poetry, "Will you walk in, my lord?" Pandarus, meanwhile, bustles around them and comments upon their progress. It seems clear that Troilus of operating on a different level of understanding than are Cressida and Pandarus—what he takes quite seriously they take casually. It is part of the "game." Cressida has declared earlier that she lies "Upon my back, to defend my belly; upon my wit, to defend my wiles" (1. 2. 282–283). She is content to think of herself as a "thing" that is prized more before it is won (1. 2. 313), and how else can one explain her behavior with Diomed unless it is assumed that she is "impure" before becoming Troilus' mistress? It is incredible to think that Troilus has corrupted her, that he has brought her to her degradation,[12] if only for naturalistic reasons; it is just as incredible as Desdemona's supposed adultery with Cassio. On the contrary, Cressida must be seen as an experienced actress in the game of love, just as everyone else in the play with the exception of Troilus is experienced at "acting" out roles without ever quite believing in them.[13] Shakespeare uses Calchas' abandonment of the Trojans to signal Cressida's coming infidelity. Just as the father betrays his native city, so does Cressida betray Troilus. Not much is made of Calchas in this play, perhaps because there are already so many characters, but Thersites does remark that he is a "traitor." In earlier treatments, Calchas, who was a Trojan bishop, is a guide and counselor for the Greeks, a respected man; in later sources he is progressively downgraded.[14] In this play he is nothing but a traitor whose flight to the Greeks brings about Cressida's actual infidelity. Not that his behavior has caused hers: Cressida could have learned infidelity from any number of sources in her world.

Troilus' tragedy is his failure to distinguish between the impulses of the body and those of the spirit. His "love" for Cressida, based upon a Platonic idea of her fairness and chastity, is a ghostly love without an object; he does not see that it would be really a lustful love based upon his desire for her body. Shakespeare is puritanical elsewhere, but I think in this play he reserves sympathy for the tragedy of the impermanence of love built upon lust; Troilus is a victim not of cunning or selfishness but simply of his own body. He may be comic in his earlier rhetorical excesses, and pathetic in his denial of Cressida's truly being Cressida (act 5, scene 2), but his predicament as a human being is certainly sympathetic. In academic criticism there is often an intolerance for any love that is not clearly spiritual, but this failure to observe the natural genesis and characteristics of love distorts the human perspective of the work of art altogether. Troilus' behavior and, indeed, his subsequent disillusionment are natural; he is not meant to be depraved, nor is his declaration of love in terms of sensual stimulation—particularly the sense of taste—meant to mark him as a hedonist and nothing more. It is Cressida, the calculating one who thinks of herself as a "thing," and Diomed, so much more clever than Troilus, who are villainous. The first line of Sonnet 151 might apply to Troilus: "Love is too young to know what conscience is." Troilus' youthful lust is a lust of innocence that tries to define itself in terms of the spiritual and the heavenly, just as Ulysses' speech on degree tries to thrust the disorderly Greeks into a metaphysical relationship to the universe and its "natural" laws. Both fail—Troilus because he does not understand his own feelings and Ulysses because there is, in fact, no relationship between man and the universe. In both failures there is the pathetic failure of man to recognize the limitations of the self and its penchant for rationalizing its desires. Nothing is ever equivalent to the energy or eloquence or love lavished upon it. Man's goals are fated to be less than his ideals would have them, and when he realizes this truth he is "enlightened" in the special sense in which tragedy enlightens men—a flash of bitter knowledge that immediately precedes death. It is difficult to believe, as Campbell argues, that the finale of *Troilus and Cressida* should be regarded only as the "intelligent use of an accepted artistic convention,"[15] that is, as the ejection of derided characters in satire, and not as the expression of personal disillusionment of these characters. Troilus is not a satisfactory tragic hero, but he is certainly a human being who has suffered an education. The fact of his going off to die in what is left of the Trojan War would seem to annul the parallel Campbell makes with the banished Malvolio of *Twelfth Night*.

The play, with its large number of characters, submits various interpretations of itself to the audience.[16] The most strident of the points of view is Thersites, who maintains one note and emerges as a kind of choral instrument to insist upon the betrayal of the spirit by the body. The violent rhythms of the play—its jagged transitions and contrasts between sweetness and bawdiness, pomposity and blunt physical action—are most obviously represented by Thersites in his labyrinth of fury. If he reminds us of anyone else in Shakespeare, it is Iago, who cannot love and who must therefore drag everyone down to his bestial level. But Thersites is more mysterious a character than Iago because he figures not at all in the action—the play would be different without him, but not radically different. He comes onto the stage and mocks the rituals that have characterized the first part of the play; we feel, after Troilus' inflamed words and the Greeks' pompous speeches, that this is a man who speaks the truth, who sees at once through all masks. Because it is static, his nihilism soon becomes wearisome. But he is not intended to be an entertaining character; he is little more than a voice that has attached itself to this war simply in order to interpret it.

Thersites makes his noisy entrance immediately after Ulysses explains his plot to get Achilles into action. He undercuts all pretensions of the council scene: if Agamemnon had boils, and the boils ran, then "would come some matter from him. I see none now." And: "There's Ulysses and old Nestor, whose wit was mouldy ere your grandsires had nails on their toes" (2. 1. 114–116). Patroclus, who is not a particularly unsympathetic character, is recognized by Thersites as Achilles' "brach," his "male varlet," and his "masculine whore." Thersites has the magical immunity and privilege of a court jester, and his fearlessness in speaking bluntly even to Achilles suggests that he is not to be explained in naturalistic terms so much as in symbolic terms. He calls for vengeance, the "Neapolitan bone-ache" on the whole camp, for this is a fitting curse for those who "war for a placket" (2. 3. 20–22). Significantly, the other character who comes closest to Thersites' cynicism is Diomed, who promises to prize Cressida according to her "worth" (4. 4. 133), and who speaks of Helen as "contaminated carrion." Because he has no illusions at all, Diomed conquers Cressida at once. Thersites' rage, however, is impotent, a rage to which no one seems to listen. He calls down curses upon

31

the heroes who surround him in an effort to deflate their fraudulent romanticism and to make them less than human. Man in Thersites' vision is a catalogue of parts; he is the maddened puritan who cannot endure the discrepancy between the ideals of man and the physical counterparts of these ideals, and who wants nothing so much as to rip to shreds the pretensions of the heroes and to substitute for their grandiose views of themselves a devastating image of man as a physical creature unable to transcend the meanness of his body. Here is Thersites in a typical curse:

. . . Now the rotten diseases of the south, the guts-griping, ruptures, catarrhs, loads o' gravel i' the back, lethargies, cold palsies, raw eyes, dirt-rotten livers, wheezing lungs, bladders full of imposthume, sciaticas, lime-kilns i' the palm, incurable bone-ache, and the rivelled fee-simple of the tetter, take and take again such preposterous discoveries! (5. 1. 20–28)

The effect of all this is exactly the opposite of that of a magical incantation. Thersites is used by Shakespeare to break illusions, to break the spells cast by the eloquent and self-deceived rhetoricians of the early scenes. He echoes Ulysses' warning that appetite will devour itself when he says "lechery eats itself" (5. 4. 37). In the scenes of battle between Troilus and Diomed, the relationship between the debased war and debased love is made clear. They take on the roles, however diminished, of Menelaus and Paris, suggesting the endlessness of infidelity. Last of all, Thersites is heard noisily excusing himself from battle:

I am a bastard too; I love bastards: I am bastard begot, bastard instructed, bastard in mind, bastard in valour, in everything illegitimate. . . . (5.7. 17–20)

He reveals himself as a coward, just as eagerly debasing himself as he has debased everyone else, and is driven off-stage with a curse: "The Devil take thee, coward!" As Tillyard remarks, the world of *Troilus and Cressida* is a world in which things happen to men, rather than a world in which men commit actions.[17] Only the evil have a positive capacity for action; the rest are powerless, and most powerless of all is Thersites in his fury.

Unlike ideal and orthodox tragedy, this play leads to no implicit affirmation of values. However, it is not necessary to say that the play gives us no "conclusion,"[18] or that it is only a "rich, varied, and interesting, indeed, heroic and sensational spectacle" devoid of clear moral significance.[19] The controversy over the genre to which the play belongs is an important one, because it suggests the complexity of the work. That it can be a comical satire to one person, a dark comedy to another, a tragedy to another, and a heroic farce to yet another makes clear the fundamental ambiguity of the work. Arguments over classification may seem superficial, but they are really concerned with the deeper, more important task of understanding the play's meaning as it is qualified by the striking extremes of tone, mockery in both content and structure, and its placing of a heroic young man in a degenerate society that seems utterly alient to him. Like Othello, with whom Brian Morris compares him,[20] Troilus is a man who is unaccountable in terms of the world that has made him: he is a "given," an innocence that is introduced only in order to be disillusioned and destroyed.

Above all, the play should be recognized as containing within itself a comment upon the "real" world and not

as a satirical offshoot of the larger world, somehow inferior to it. It does not point toward another, better, more
perfect way of living. This is important or we will interpret the play as satire against courtly love and chivalric
ideals. It is certainly a satire against these codes of living,
but it is also much more; like *Gulliver's Travels*, it works
toward establishing all mankind as its satiric object.
There has been much discussion about Shakespeare's
reasons for choosing this familiar story, but I think it important to insist that the play's world—like the worlds of
the tragedies—is complete within itself. It is a mythic or
allegorical representation of a complete action that does
not demand outside knowledge to fufill it. R. A. Foakes
suggests that we see or experience the play in a kind of
"double time," seeing beyond the moment and knowing
more than the characters do at any particular point:

. . . if [Shakespeare] reduces the accepted stature of the
heroes . . . he does it securely in the knowledge that we will
have in mind the legend that has descended from Homer,
via Virgil, with medieval accretions . . . and has survived
all additions and modifications to maintain still the ready
image of Hector and Achilles as types of great warriors, Helen
as a type of beauty. This vision modifies our attitude to the
play. . . .[21]

This idea, while imaginative and stimulating, is based
upon an erroneous conception of what drama is. We
must remember that the play is meant to be played,
shown, demonstrated, and that while a work of art is unfolding, no observer, however learned, can experience it
with a "double awareness." This is certainly to attach too
great an agility to the mind. I believe that Shakespeare in
this instance seized upon a popular story in order to use
it, simply, as a symbolic representation of an idea that at

this time of his life must have obsessed him, and that the Troilus-Cressida story and the Trojan War story are not meant to be played out against anyone's prior knowledge but are intended to transcend or negate this prior knowledge, or simply to create another world altogether—just as someone like Faulkner is obsessed with a Christ-pattern in his works, not in order to derive meaning from a comparison with the biblical Christ but rather to substitute for that Christ a "real" Christ, a human being. This makes the difference between merely clever art based upon cultural knowledge of earlier art (one certainly thinks of T. S. Eliot in this respect) and art that is deadly serious and wants to absolutely re-create and reinterpret the world. There can be nothing "left over" in *Troilus and Cressida*, and Shakespeare works hard to establish our attitude to his play through his relentless imagery and irony—he would not be secure in the knowledge that our attitudes were going to be modified by other versions of the legend.

Laurence Michel, centering his analysis on *Othello*, sees Shakespearean tragedy as a "critique of humanism from the inside." [22] He studies the discrepancy between the pretensions of humanism and the stark reality of tragedy, which sees "everything humanistically worthwhile . . . blighted, then irretrievably cracked; men are made mad, and then destroyed. . . ." Following Aristotle's insistence upon the primacy of the plot, Michel suggests that the plot, as the soul of the action, criticizes the humanistic ideals that the characters live by, and that this is therefore a critique from the "inside." *Troilus and Cressida*, so much more complex than *Othello*, suggests by its subject matter and its mockery of opposites (flawed "reason" vs. flawed "emotion") a criticism of the pretensions of tragedy itself—whether it is redefined as "metatheater" or simply as flawed tragedy. The constant ironic undercutting of appearances; the fragments of tragic action that never quite achieve tragedy; above all, the essential philosophic split between the realm of the eternal and that of the existential, the temporarily existing, make it a comment on man's relationship to himself that is very nearly contemporary. More than any other play of Shakespeare's, it is *Troilus and Cressida* about which Auerbach seems to be speaking when he discusses the radical differences between the tragedies of Shakespeare and those of antiquity.[23]

2

THE TRAGEDY OF IMAGINATION: Shakespeare's "Antony and Cleopatra"

Nature wants stuff
To vie strange forms with fancy . . .
—*Antony and Cleopatra*

Shakespeare's *Antony and Cleopatra* shares with *Troilus and Cressida* the obsessive and self-consuming rage of the tragic figure as he confronts and attempts to define "reality." But, more extravagantly than *Troilus and Cressida*, this reality is layered with masquerade; forms that are often as lyric as brutal shift and change and baffle expectation. The constant refinement of brute reality into lyric illusion is the work not simply of Antony, Shakespeare's hero, but the lifelong work of Shakespeare himself. Thus there is a curious, rather decadent air in this play of flamboyant desires having as much import— if not ultimately as much political strength—as events themselves. Lionel Abel states that among the characters of *Hamlet* there are four playwrights: Claudius, the Ghost, Polonius, and Hamlet.[1] Among the characters of *Anthony and Cleopatra* there are any number of mythologizing poets and/or playwrights, but the most important is Antony. Snared within the net of appearances and forced by politics (that most extreme form of fantasy) to break free, Antony's agony is curiously muted for someone who has achieved and lost so much; but this fact can be better understood if we examine the basis of the play and its relationship to "tragedy."

The movement of most works of literature—whether the simple medieval morality play or the ambiguous *Troilus and Cressida*—is toward a dramatic confrontation with reality, with objective truth. The hero's downfall (or, in happier works, his conversion or enlightenment) is determined by the success with which reality overcomes appearances. If there is any great theme of literature this is it: the destruction of the *faux-semblant* and attendant illusions by the intervention, bitter or glorious, of reality. Tragedy works with this theme and is inseparable from it, and the problem of *Antony and Cleopatra* seems to be that the lovers either do not have illusions or, if they do, they never learn to substitute for them other visions of their predicament, in the classical way that Creon of Sophocles' *Antigone* does, or in the way Othello and Macbeth do. Orthodox and recognizable tragedy necessarily involves a process of learning and exorcism, which is manipulated by the tragic figure himself, as in *Oedipus Rex*, or by surrounding characters who may or may not be fragmented aspects of the hero himself, as in *The Revenger's Tragedy*, or by fate or external social forces, as in Ibsen's *Ghosts*. In *Antony and Cleo-*

40

patra all exorcism fails: just as Antony cannot rid himself of his obsession with Cleopatra, so Cleopatra cannot quite rid herself of the earth-bound and, in a crude sense, comic aspects of her own mortality. Exorcism works to dispel illusion, but the poetry of *Antony and Cleopatra* works to create illusion. The play is sustained by words alone, for its plot is certainly incidental; we are never interested in what a character does, but only in how he expresses his consciousness of what he has done, and what this evokes in the mirroring rhetoric of his witnesses. Here reality does not defeat appearances; appearances are made— through a pressure that approaches magic—to defeat reality or at least render it irrelevant.

Comedy also traditionally penetrates illusions; it is the incongruity of what is supposed and what is that produces laughter. But *Antony and Cleopatra* relates most immediately and most helpfully to comedy, since its tragic dimensions are attained (in acts 4 and 5) by an excess and concentration of emotion that is not anticipated in the earlier acts. The first act is comic in intention: the lovers insist upon their love's hyperbole and most specifically upon Antony's rejection of his former life. In a pretense of negatives, he states his real concerns:

> Let Rome in Tiber melt, and the wide arch
> Of the rang'd empire fall! Here is my space.
> Kingdoms are clay; our dungy earth alike
> Feeds beast as man.
>
> (1. 1. 33–36)

At the end of the act he leaves for Rome to strengthen his hold on the empire and to escape Egyptian "dotage." The banter and play acting of the first scene show Antony and Cleopatra at their worst, and this self-caricatur-

41

ing, since it cannot be so judged until much later, gives a credulity to the opening speech that would not ordinarily belong to it. This is Philo's judgment of Antony, which may be equated exactly with the judgment of the Roman world: Antony is the "triple pillar of the world transform'd/ Into a strumpet's fool" (1. 1. 12–13). The paradoxical nature of Antony's infatuation is vividly suggested by these lines:

> His captain's heart,
> Which in the scuffles of great fights hath burst
> The buckles on his breast, reneges all temper,
> And is become the bellows and the fan
> To cool a gipsy's lust.
>
> (1. 1. 6–10)

The surrender of the militant must constitute for the Romans an unqualified surrender; the problem for the spectator or reader is the extent to which Roman judgment may be trusted. But the central image here works for the Antony of the entire play: what is unforgettable in this Antony is his "heart" on any level, the organ of courage, of magnanimity, of loyalty, of love, of hysterical valor possible only by a "diminution in [his] brain." Antony *is* his heart, as Caesar is his reason, and the heart, being blind, may understand the complexities of the "tawny front" (Philo's description of Cleopatra) by other means. The "front" has its obvious irony in that Antony is a military man; it has its obvious accusation in that it is but a mask, a façade; but not so obvious is the fact that, since it is a façade, there may be dimensions enjoyed by it that would baffle the Roman mind. The image works, then, in two directions, and the Roman Philo, speaking scornfully, is allowed to say more than he means. Antony's heart, apparently having met defeat on this battle front, has become a bellows, so retaining its pulsing, contracting and expanding motions, but having undergone a metamorphosis that cannot be admired. The paradox is that the bellows and the fan which "cool a gipsy's lust" do not cool but enflame; their purpose, as instruments, is to do so. The image of the cyclical cooling and enflaming, then, can suggest that fluctuating course Antony will follow, and, in its apparent preoccupation with a single object, the man himself: a man of complexity, a colossus and a ruffian who consumes himself in the love that, by devouring him, transforms him into a being the military Antony, noble as he might be, could not imagine. The image suggests, further, a shameful helplessness; it suggests entrapment, the commitment of the passionate being to his passion, but never the commitment of the passive being to his "fate." Common judgments of Antony are perplexed, or at best mixed. He is not a tragic figure in any recognizable sense; he may yearn for "the love of Love, and her soft hours" in act 1, but in act 4, at death, he will not yearn for more than this.

The bantering first scene is followed by an interlude of sophisticated joking among lesser people—Cleopatra's servants and the Roman friend of Antony, Enobarbus. The cliché of the anticipation of death in the midst of life, or luxurious gaiety, and the prophecies of the soothsayer are as close in *Antony and Cleopatra* as one comes to the conventionalities of tragedy. Does this argue for supernatural design or is it introduced to strengthen, structurally, the meandering energy of the play? Later Antony's god, Hercules, will desert him (in Plutarch, it is Bacchus), but Antony registers no consciousness of this symbolic act. It does not work—as do the garden scene of

43

Richard II or the scene in *Troilus and Cressida* in which
Hector slaughters the strange knight "for his hide"—to relate directly to the hero's interpretation of his plight or to
add to the audience's understanding of its dimensions. It
is eerie; it is mystical; it is a possibility—just as anything
in the enchanted Egypt is a possibility—but its suggestion of divine force or fate is never taken up by anyone in
the play. *Antony and Cleopatra* is the most godless of
Shakespeare's plays, because it is about human beings for
whom anything less than self-divinity will be failure.

It is not only Cleopatra who suggests a mysterious variety, but Antony as well. Much as he reveals himself in
his words, his half-false sincerities and his half-truthful
lies, there is mystery in him because he is in a process of
change. His variety is suggested by the differing men who
see him, and, most famously, by Cleopatra after his
death. To his officer, Ventidius, he is a captain generous
only to those who keep themselves, cautiously and
wisely, inferior to him (act 3, scene 1); to Enobarbus he
is a "fool" (3. 11. 42) and yet a "mine of bounty" for
whom one might give his life (4. 6. 32); to Caesar, the
Antony of old was a great soldier who fought "with pa-
tience more/ Than savages could suffer" (1. 4. 60–61),
but who is now "a man who is the abstract of all faults/
That all men follow" (1. 4. 9–10). Caesar might have
gone on to see that Antony is not flawed by his faults but
is his faults; in him, as in Cleopatra, the vilest things become themselves. Yet to Lepidus, there are not "evils
enow to darken all his goodness;/ His faults in him seem
as the spots of heaven,/ More fiery by night's blackness"
(1. 4. 11–13). Antony is to be considered, frequently, in
terms of light and dark imagery; what is perplexing is the
ease with which the polar values of light and dark may be

44

confused. Antony "is," in Cleopatra's famous speech, light itself: he is the sun and the moon and the heavens. Yet his faults in him seem as the spots (stars) of heaven —again light, and perhaps the same light. This cosmic light blinks good and evil; when one leaves the atmosphere of the human condition, the two become indistinguishable.

But Caesar's point here is earthbound:

> If he fill'd
> His vacancy with his voluptuousness,
> Full surfeits and the dryness of his bones
> Call on him for 't; but to confound such time
> That drums him from his sport, and speaks as loud
> As his own state and ours, 'tis to be chid.
>
> (1. 4. 25–30)

The tension in *Antony and Cleopatra* is, clearly, not between good and evil and not between appearances and reality. It is simply between two views of the world, the Roman and the Egyptian, the cold Machiavellianism of those who deal in lieutenantry (3. 9. 39) and the unfixed, pulsating, undignified voluptuousness of those to whom passion has become a world. I speak of tension, but really this contention between opposites counts for little more than the formal plot. There is never any doubt about the impending victory of reason—if it is a victory; the tension is not, as in *Troilus and Cressida*, exploited as mock tension and made to demonstrate the shabbiness of both love-worshiping Trojans and reason-worshiping Greeks. In *Antony and Cleopatra* both ways of viewing the world are given generous consideration, the final point being that they are simply different and that any one world threatens or suffers opposing worlds.

45

The one necessarily moves out of itself, bent upon conquering; the other moves in upon itself and draws the world in after, so that to the great soldier Antony, the absurdity of challenging Caesar to a duel is never recognizable. The political must resist emotions, though they may trade upon them; the passionate recognize only emotions, though they may recognize at the same time their serious limitations. What is interesting is that for both species of man, faith in appearances supercedes faith in reality, or it may be that, for both, appearances turn into reality.

Thus the sacrifice of the limpid Octavia: Caesar and Antony cannot understand each other, and do not want to, but their accustomed faith in ceremony meets in the proposal of the political marriage between Antony and Octavia. They are role-takers; therefore, we feel no distaste for Antony as he dismisses his love of Cleopatra as "poison'd hours," since we know he does not tell the truth but speaks only ceremonially. We take our cues in the play from Enobarbus, the plain dealer who is out of place in this meeting:

. . . if you borrow one another's love for the instant, you may, when you hear no more words of Pompey, return it again: you shall have time to wrangle in when you have nothing else to do.

(2.2. 107–111)

Enobarbus pretends not to understand the decorum of this world. Instead, the doomed Lepidus interprets it: "Her love to both/ Would each to other and all loves to both/ Draw after her" (2. 2. 141–143). History is too fraudulent to be telescoped into anything but comedy. So Antony, newly contracted to Caesar through the political marriage, recognizes no change in relationships but, inspired by the catalytic words of the soothsayer, foresees his doom in Caesar's alienness:

> The very dice obey him.
> And in our sports my better cunning faints
> Under his chance.
> . . . .
> And though I make this marriage for my peace,
> I' the east my pleasure lies.
>
> (2. 3. 33–40)

The relationship of Antony and Cleopatra is as apparently ignoble as nobility will allow. We see them as lovers in fragments: they wander through the streets and "note the qualities of people"; they lie brilliantly and passionately to each other; they swear their love in impossibly exaggerated terms; they do not trust each other. Above all, they are not youthful lovers: Cleopatra sees herself as "with Phoebus' amorous pinches black,/ And wrinkled deep in time" (1. 5. 28–29); Antony speaks angrily of sending to "the boy Caesar . . . this grizzled head" (3. 11. 17). But in them surface conventions and the reality of spirit are blurred, as the good and evil of Antony become one in the dazzling light he embodies. So Cleopatra, with "wann'd" lip, is still the queen of her exotic land, and is evoked in the famous set-piece in which Enobarbus describes her to an awe-stricken Roman as an impression rather than a reality—and it is the impression, finally, that matters. The scene upon the barge—the air love-sick with perfume, the rich imagery of gold and purple and silver, the transformation of attendants into cupids and mermaids, most of all the transformation of the perhaps desperate Cleopatra into

47

Venus—may just miss being absurd; delivered by a Thersites, this would come to us differently. But Enobarbus, whose sense of reality we are to trust, understands that she does "make defect perfection" and that, given this alchemy, the logical Roman world and its judgments are irrelevant. The paradox Cleopatra embodies is suggested most succinctly in Agrippa's exclamation, "Royal wench!" Cleopatra's majesty is such that so crude a comic scene as the one in which she assaults the messenger of ill news does not destroy it; she is described in terms of food and eating, and describes herself so, but this counts, ultimately, as one of the symptoms of her complexity and not simply of her baseness. Recurring in her, even at her death, is a propensity to view matters comically.

History as possible comedy (when enacted, as it must be, by mortal men) is one of the motifs of *Antony and Cleopatra*; it comes out most successfully abroad Pompey's galley (act 2, scene 7), where the pillars of the world end their banquet in a drunken communion that means, of course, nothing. The Roman disposition is more recognizably admirable than the Egyptian, because it is normally ambitious. But in the end it is no more meaningful, and its ceremonies, though usually sober, come to the same thing as the illusion of the cupids and mermaids attending their scheming Venus. *Antony and Cleopatra* is as ceremonial a play as *Richard II* and *Troilus and Cressida*, but though all ceremonies come to nothing finally, the abandonment of these forms in *Antony and Cleopatra* does not constitute the education it does in the other plays; realizing the sham of ceremonies is quite equivalent to realizing the sham of one's self and the world. If there is a difference between what the world (at its crudest, biological) suggests and what ceremony demands, then it is clearly the world that must be abandoned, since it becomes "no better than a sty." This is the curious point: suicide here is an escape from the disappointing world, but not an escape from the self, whose nobility is never diminished.

The people of both worlds, Roman and Egyptian, live according to ceremony. Enobarbus dies out of grief at the fulfillment of a ritual of friendship, when Antony sends his treasure and more after him; indeed, his death itself is ceremonial. Caesar, disgusted, may scorn Antony's vulgar performance when Antony at last flees back to Egypt:

> I' the market-place, on a tribunal silver'd,
> Cleopatra and himself in chairs of gold
> Were publicly enthron'd; at the feet sat
> Caesarion, whom they call my father's son,
> And all the unlawful issue that their lust
> Since then hath made between them.
> . . . .
> I' the common show-place, where they exercise.
>   (3. 6. 3–12)

But he will, minutes later, attack bitterly the manner of his sister's arrival because it has not enough of show in it:

>   You come not
> Like Caesar's sister; the wife of Antony
> Should have an army for an usher, and
> The neighs of horse to tell of her approach
> Long ere she did appear; the trees by the way
> Should have borne men; and expectation fainted,
> Longing for what it had not.
> . . . .

> But you are come
> A market-maid to Rome, and have prevented
> The ostentation of our love, which, left unshown,
> Is often left unlov'd.
>
> (3. 6. 42–53)

There is no distinction on this level between the Roman and the Egyptian: reality loses itself in appearance.

Later Antony, preparing for his suicide, will dream of his reunion with Cleopatra after death in terms of this "show." It is not enough for the lovers to dwell together in romantic bliss for eternity; their love exists, clearly enough, at least in part in the awe of witnesses:

> Where souls do couch on flowers, we'll hand in hand,
> And with our sprightly port make the ghosts gaze;
> Dido and her Aeneas shall want troops,
> And all the haunt be ours.
>
> (4. 12. 51–54)

This does not substract from their love, but rather qualifies it as a particular sort of love that gives more of itself to supposed irrelevancies than romantic love can afford to surrender. This love is not orthodox, and so it is suspect; it has always been suspect in regard to Cleopatra. After the defeat at Actium, however, with their world shaken and its vastness for the first time questioned, Antony and Cleopatra become recognizably human. Ceremony is forgotten in the urgency of the moment, and they are reconciled, though the loyal Enobarbus, the spokesman or chorus for the action, has lost his faith in the world of passion and its excesses: one must simply "think, and die" (3. 11. 2). Enobarbus' reason tells him to abandon his failing master, envisioned as a dangerous, dying old lion, but if we have assumed Enobarbus' wisdom, we are forced at his death to assume also his guilt. He dies of disloyalty, and the fact of disloyalty is in itself sinful, despite the important fact that "loyalty well held to fools does make . . . faith mere folly" (3. 11. 42). The several climaxes of the play baffle expectation. If the processes of exorcism are to be completed, Antony as the deluded lover must collide with reality and must see his folly. But the movement toward tragic enlightenment is always thwarted, and Antony withdraws from these encounters with his faith in his condition untouched. So after the battle at Actium when Antony seems a defeated man—"I am so lated in the world that I / Have lost my way for ever" (3. 9. 3)—it is not the temptation of suicide that masters him but the totality of his commitment to Cleopatra. He is able to say:

> Fall not a tear, I say; one of them rates
> All that is won and lost.
> . . . .
>   Love, I am full of lead.
> Some wine, within there, and our viands! Fortune knows,
> We scorn her most when most she offers blows.
>   (3. 9. 69–74)

So he makes his early speech about his indifference to worldly fortune come true.

The next climax comes when Antony sees Caesar's messenger kissing Cleopatra's hand; he does not see that she is acting a part. His judgment on her turns back upon himself in a passage that should work as a catharsis of his love and his bondage:

> . . . when we in our viciousness grow hard,—
> O misery on 't!—the wise gods seel our eyes;
> In our own filth drop our clear judgments; make us

Adore our errors; laugh at 's, while we strut
To our confusion.

(3. 11. 111–115)

He is maddened by Caesar's "harping on what I am, /
Not what he knew I was" as if his life were over. But he
is again reconciled to Cleopatra, whose dignity grows
when his diminishes, and believes they will yet do well.
Enobarbus sees Antony as so furious that he is "frighted
out of fear," and consequently not the old Antony. His
bravado has a new sound of hollowness:

I will be treble-sinew'd, hearted, breath'd,
And fight maliciously; for when mine hours
Were nice and lucky, men did ransom lives
Of me for jests; but now I'll set my teeth,
And send to darkness all that stop me. Come,
Let's have one other gaudy night: call to me
All my sad captains.

(3. 11. 177–183)

The apparent change of fortune that follows (they
beat back Caesar's men) makes the final catastrophe the
more complete.

After the last defeat, when Cleopatra's men desert to
the enemy, Antony is brought to a revelation of what
reality is for him, but again this revelation is discarded.
The apparent betrayal of Cleopatra constitutes a betrayal
of all appearance:

Sometimes we see a cloud that's dragonish;
A vapour sometime like a bear or lion . . .

. . . .
                    Thou hast seen these signs;
They are black vesper's pageants. . . .
That which is now a horse, even with a thought

The rack dislimns, and makes it indistinct,
As water is in water.

(4. 12. 2–11)

The protean condition of man and his world, a vision presented here with deadly vividness, is offset for Antony only by the false report that Cleopatra has killed herself. His commitment to love is again realized, and he prepares for death. It is the final restoration of faith in love that justifies the expenditure of passion the play has permitted. Death is neither escape nor self-punishment; it is, of course, a mistake, yet it is at the same time a willful surrender to something very like love. Eros is Antony's knave and Antony's god: Antony will "make death love me" and will "run into 't/ As to a lover's bed." Brutus dies because he has awakened from delusion; Othello dies when freed from the delusion of what he is; Troilus, not a tragic figure, perhaps, nevertheless goes into battle to die when confronted with the prospect of a world totally corrupted. But Antony dies with his faith in love renewed. This long death scene avoids a ghastly sentimentality partially by Cleopatra's unromantic wariness (fearing capture, she will not leave the monument to come to the dying Antony), partially by the confidence with which the lovers affirm themselves and their love, partially by the sheer hyperbolic force of the poetry itself.

The play is conceived in hyperbole, the controlled hysteria of Renaissance language to which no world was ever equal. If the confines of this Roman-Egyptian world are not admittedly fake, then they are, by necessity, without limitation. The known world is collapsed into Antony, Cleopatra, and Caesar; nothing is missing from it, since they combine among them all its brilliance and its stupidity. Antony can say of himself that with his sword he "quarter'd the world" (4. 12. 58); Cleopatra can say of him—beginning the extended creation and re-creation of her lover that must be unmatched in literature for its audacity and beauty—that he destroys with himself all order in the world: "Young boys and girls/ Are level now with men; the odds is gone,/ And there is nothing left remarkable/ Beneath the visiting moon" (4. 13. 65–68). Even Caesar can say "the death of Antony/ Is not a single doom; in the name lay/ A moiety of the world" (5. 1. 16–18). The play is finally Antony's, for Cleopatra is priestess to his apotheosis in the speech toward which all earlier poetry moves:

> His legs bestrid the ocean; his rear'd arm
> Crested the world; his voice was propertied
> As all the tuned spheres, and that to friends;
> But when he meant to quail and shake the orb,
> He was as rattling thunder. For his bounty,
> There was no winter in 't, an autumn 'twas
> That grew the more by reaping; his delights
> Were dolphin-like, they show'd his back above
> The element they liv'd in; in his livery
> Walk'd crowns and crownets, realms and islands were
> As plates dropp'd from his pocket.
>
> (5. 2. 82–92)

The wonder of these flights of poetry is that they seem to give nothing of their certainty to the ceremony of the earlier acts of the play. If it is not possible that Antony was as he is dreamed, then it is not the lapsed Antony this play is about. If their "strength is all gone into heaviness," this heaviness testifies simply for the magnitude of that former strength that has now destroyed itself. Antony's death teaches Cleopatra the vanity of life, subject to fortune; the betrayal of her treasurer renders this education immediately suspect, just as the knowledge that Caesar will lead her in triumph obscures forever Cleopatra's motives for dying. Shakespeare balances hyperbole with comic suggestion: the Antony as colossus and the Antony as ruffian, the Cleopatra equal to all visions of herself and the Cleopatra raging at the servant who has betrayed her. But the counterpoint does not work here—as it does, for instance, in *Dr. Faustus* with its vaudeville scenes of Wagner playing magician—to qualify the grandeur of these people and to cheat them of their incredible dignity. Instead, it works to suggest by contrast the range of behavior this dignity allows itself, and the heights to which it succeeds. Thus Cleopatra becomes unforgettable precisely because she is a woman, and at times a small woman; what is insisted upon is her humanity, the ascent of angels or demonic gods being too easy. The baseness of Cleopatra does not preclude her greatness but assures it, since without this her presence would be no more than a flight of words. This magic, admittedly, will not work for everyone. Though the modern temperament admires passion and individuality more than the older virtues of prudence, modesty, and chastity, Cleopatra may still be interpreted as Shakespeare's Romans see her, and Antony's death may be seen as simply the necessary result of his having surrendered his reason to immoral passion. But the magic works for Antony and Cleopatra, and it need not do more.

The denial of prosaic reality and its metamorphosis into something rich and strange are possible through the language Shakespeare uses. Thus the chilling vision Antony has of the cloud formations that baffle the eye and that extend, in their impermanence, into the lives of men

55

is a vision that may be utilized profitably by the victims of this world of appearances. Antony dies with his belief in Cleopatra and himself secure (and it is surely Shakespeare's Antony that William Carlos Williams has in mind in his whimsical poem, "To Mark Anthony in Heaven," the sense of the poem being that Antony's experience and his commitment to love are "heaven," man's highest achievement). Cleopatra asks, after her envisioning of Antony as a colossus, whether there was such a man as that of whom she speaks; when told there was not, she replies:

> You lie, up to the hearing of the gods.
> But, if there be, or ever were, one such,
> It's past the size of dreaming; nature wants stuff
> To vie strange forms with fancy; yet to imagine
> An Antony were nature's piece 'gainst fancy,
> Condemning shadows quite.
>
> (5. 2. 94–99)

This condemnation of "shadows" is the metaphorical basis upon which the entire play works. These lines propose a question they do not answer, since by the choice of words (nature "imagines") the meaning is made ambiguous. Clearly there has been an Antony, and there is doubt about his being past the size of dreaming, but— and this is the irony—if there has been this Antony, it is the highest achievement of nature's own imagining, or creating; it falls beyond man's capacity for understanding. At her own death Cleopatra is able to transform by her imagination the snake to a "baby asleep at my breast,/ That sucks the nurse asleep," this final alchemy no more wonderful than that which has lighted the entire play. We must turn to a Prospero to encounter equal omnipotence.

56

It is reality that is defeated in this play, and its defeat goes unmourned. The uses of poetry are nowhere in Shakespeare so well imagined as in this work about godly creatures who delight in their humanity, and who leave their traces upon all corners of their gigantic world. Illusion could not be sustained in Hamlet's gloomy Denmark, or on the wild fields of Scotland; it requires the light-drenched world of old Egypt, a world that exists nowhere except in this play and then only within its words, by the strenuous magic of its language. In Shakespeare's works after *Antony and Cleopatra*, language will expand its uses to become both "action" and "theme," moving toward the purely lyric.

3

MELVILLE
and the Tragedy
of Nihilism

Like Shakespeare, Melville is obsessed with the fragmentary and deceiving nature of "reality"; unlike Shakespeare, he is obsessed as well with the relationship of man to God. Melville's God can take any shape, being magically and evilly empowered—He is a primitive God, related to or actually contained in a beast; He is an intellectual God, existing only in the imagination of man; He is a God of all that is antihuman, perhaps the Devil himself. Melville felt most passionately about the role of the artist, that highest type of man—here is the statement he makes after having read Hawthorne:

61

There is the grand truth about Nathaniel Hawthorne. He says No! in thunder; but the Devil himself cannot make him say *yes*. For all men who say *yes* lie; and all men who say *no* —why, they are in the happy condition of the judicious unencumbered travellers . . . they cross the frontiers into Eternity with nothing but a carpet-bag—that is to say, the Ego.[1]

The artist becomes a kind of antipriest, a naysayer in the face of all illusion. Certainly he is a guardian of the blackest of truths, for Melville felt that no intelligent mind is ever detached from the concepts of "innate depravity" and "original sin." In his essay on Melville in the popular *The American Novel and Its Tradition* Richard Chase fixes Melville's world as "insolubly dualistic": man cannot transcend his finite situation, and wavers between the antipodal forces of good and evil, heaven and hell, God and Satan, head and heart, spirit and matter.[2]

This naysaying Melville seems impossible to reconcile with the general tone of his last work, *Billy Budd*—that strange, exhausted, flawed tragedy, a work of fiction only partway imagined, in which Melville's powerful rhetoric tries vainly to do the work of his imagination. The problem of *Billy Budd*—its role as a "testament of acceptance" or a pure, dispassionate rejection of the accidental or humanly manipulated injustice of life—is a critical problem that, on the level of an assumed antithesis in its conception, will never be solved. The "dualism" Chase sees in Melville's world has become, perhaps, a dualism for the critic as well. But the problem of the place of *Billy Budd* in Melville's work and the more general, and less obvious, problem of Melville's attitude toward art, life, and nature are not insoluble, at least not unapproachable, if the current critical appeal to Melville—

usually as the basis upon which to work out more general phases of American literature—is recognized as not consistent in Melville himself, and, in fact, not borne out by his later major writings.

The "No! in thunder" describes well a youthful climate of mind found in such an early work as *White Jacket* (1850). White Jacket, arraigned at the mast, about to be flogged, is overwhelmed by the thought of escape: he could murder his captain and commit suicide. He thinks:

> I felt my man's manhood so bottomless within me that no word, no blow, no scourge . . . would cut me deep enough . . . I but swung to an instinct in me—the instinct diffused through all animated nature, that same that prompts even a worm to turn under the heel.[3]

White Jacket is saved at the last moment from this instinct. His rebellion is not transformed into action, and he will say, later, when the man-of-war world approaches harbor:

> Let us leave the ship on the sea—still with the land out of sight—still with the brooding darkness on the face of the deep. I love an indefinite, infinite background—a vast, heaving, rolling, mysterious rear! (p. 373)

The "infinite background" of *White Jacket* is the ocean of a romanticism that is, somehow, always pure in spite of its experience with, and frequent obsession with, the forces of "evil." It must not be considered a romanticism that would eclipse a vision of evil such as Melville has already expressed as early as *Typee*, but rather a romanticism that sees past the existential to the essential, beyond the immediate suffering in man to his capacity for new experience, new roles, an invasion into the universe, perhaps even a masculine victory. The tone of

63

White Jacket, for all its social protest, is one of an irrepressible optimism: the optimism that grows out of a faith in one's self and in the solidarity of man as a species, without which the "no" one cries against the devil would be meaningless.

The most famous naysayer of American literature, Captain Ahab, inhabits a world of an "infinite background," which is intolerably hidden from him by the masks of physical reality. Yet it is a temptation to him because he wills it to be so; the nightmare of *Moby Dick* (the annihilation of man by an utterly devastating nature) is not without redemption for us because we are made to understand continually that the quest, whether literal or metaphysical, need not be taken. Man chooses this struggle. The doom that overturns upon the human constituents of the drama is a doom that they, as willful human beings, insist upon: for Ahab does insist upon his doom. The choice has been made, and action may seem compulsive in the present; the weaving ball of "free will" surrenders to the fateful cry from the whaleman's lookout, yet this is still a compulsiveness that is self-inspired, a creation of the ego. And, in the end, it is not really deceived. The grandeur of human consciousness, even of futility, gives us the sense of a choice of nightmares.

When Ahab says:

"What is it, what nameless, inscrutable, unearthly thing is it, what . . . cruel, remorseless emperor commands me; that against all natural lovings and longings, I so keep pushing, and crowding, and jamming myself on all the time . . . ? Is Ahab, Ahab? Is it I, God, or who, that lifts this arm?"

he is calling upon secret yet somehow knowable patterns of reality that sustain his world, and his hatred for this

64

world. Ahab's monomania does not exclude a recognition of his confusing role in the drama—is he Ahab, or is "Ahab" someone else? What is his identity? Does he exist as an autonomous being or is he merely the acting-out of a decree of another will? His consciousness of his own futility, at times, suggests that he is a tragic hero of a new type—one who knowingly and willingly chooses his "fate," however mistaken this may seem to others. He is a romantic hero, in relation to the white whale as Milton's Satan is to God, an alternately raging, alternating despairing rebel against the supreme order. The human victim within such a tautology is a victim who demands disaster; we feel that if the personified universe did not destroy him, he would have to destroy himself. Yet an important distinction between Melville and Milton must be made: while Milton gives us the godly side of the struggle for man and leaves the reader no doubt as to the ultimate meaning of *Paradise Lost*, Melville gives us only man's side, and his constant tone is one of ambiguity. A tragedy of ambiguous meanings is a modern tragedy, in which certain classical remnants appear amid the chaos of a post-Copernican universe.

Ahab does surely say "No," and he would say it to God as well as the Devil. Unfortunately, God is no more present than the Devil—in fact, God is less present than the Devil. Ahab has created a world of an irreconcilable dualism in which he not only believes, but to which he has surrendered himself; without this terrific dualism—without his religious faith in it—he would topple from the height of a pseudo-god to the level of the merely human. The merely human is a condition in which, perhaps, the voicing of a "No" to the universe is not only futile but without meaning. Up to this point in Melville's works,

65

and a little beyond, the emphasis upon the "No," upon the dualism and the blackness as evil, is surely legitimate. These central passions are the catalysts for the inner rage of the works, and their relationship to similar themes in American literature is certainly valuable to criticism. Though to Lewis Mumford it seems that Melville "conquered the white whale in his own consciousness" [4] through the creation of *Moby Dick*, the appearance of *Pierre* in the following year would suggest that few problems had really been worked out, that even more had been discovered. *Pierre* is the tale of a quest on land that, like Ahab's on sea, is to lead to a confrontation of "truth" and a definition of the self measured by this truth—ideally; it should lead to a victory and a rejection of the conventional world of social and physical and psychological arrangements. The movement in the novel is away from the appearance of things to the penetration of a supposed reality; it is a concern for the definition of this reality, a qualification of truth by endless ambiguities in the self as well as in the world. Thus the novel seems a psychological fantasy, where the will of the hero creates events in the way in which an author creates: Pierre wishes for a sister, and the sister miraculously appears; Pierre wishes for an "objective" justification of his seemingly idealistic, Christlike behavior, and the pamphlet on "Chronometrical and Horologicals" appears; Pierre wishes for a neutralizing of his passion for his suspected half sister, Isabel—or perhaps a salvation from the necessity of dealing with it responsibly—and his "good" angel, Lucy, arrives to live with them. Pierre, in rejecting the horological life (the compromising, accommodating life), believes that he is giving himself to truth. This is identified with the heart as against the head, the pure

66

passion against the corrupting intellect. So far as Pierre's rejection of appearance is sincere, and even so far as his gradual awareness of the ambiguity within his own heart is considered in terms of a real dichotomy between good and evil, Pierre belongs to the sphere of the pre-Adamic figure turned Adamic and fallen, in turn changed to the Faustian figure somewhat akin to Ahab—that is, a man involved in a real struggle with appearance and reality, good and evil, God and Satan. The casual linking of these archetypal roles suggests the extent to which Melville, like many "modern" writers, thinks in terms of mythical role-taking; but where in the hands of a less talented writer these figures could turn into empty allegorical abstractions, Melville gives life to the abstractions themselves, dramatizing the plight of the Adamic man who loses his innocence and is precipitated to an immediate Faustian hubris and audacity.

The human heart (the human "unconscious") is always an enigma, but it can be read as no more than the superficial confusion of an underlying order, an essential pattern that the seeker must discover. Pierre says:

"Is it possible, after all, that spite of bricks and shaven faces, this world we live in is brimmed with wonders, and I and all mankind, beneath our garbs of commonplaceness, conceal enigmas that the stars themselves, and perhaps the highest seraphim cannot resolve?" [5]

The presence of the enigma does not indicate any movement of Pierre beyond Ahab: it is the assumption itself, and even the form of the question, that asserts Pierre's confused faith in at least the ultimate order of nature. But it is the beginning of a profound metaphysical doubt. He will search, on his pilgrimage, for the "talismanic secret" to reconcile that world with his heart, but he will find only silence—"that profound Silence, that only Voice of our God" (p. 290).

From the ambiguity of his small cloistered world to the ambiguity of the outer world and, finally, to the ambiguity of his own "pure" and unquestioned motives, Pierre is led to the discovery of a world of lies. It is not only a world that tells lies but a world that has been committed—created—in lies. The questioning of Pierre's own motives in protecting Isabel provides one of the most interesting of the novel's ambiguities, for even the motif of incest will not serve as an adequate explanation of sorts for the conflict of the novel. While it can be assumed that the gradual awareness of an incestuous desire for his "sister" comes to Pierre to typify both the ambiguity of the world and his own corrupted purity, the incest-motif might not be the concern or fear of the protagonist at all, but rather its opposite: he is really afraid of a healthy and normal love relationship. Perhaps the suspicion of incest is a protective device, and so far as it does keep Pierre "pure" in the obvious sense in which Billy Budd is pure, and even Roderick Usher is pure, it is a device that works successfully. The incompatibility of innocence and even normal experience in American literature is never surprising, but its manifestations can assume at times monstrous distortions. It is as if an act of heretical blasphemy were somehow less shameful than the most natural physical act.

On another level, the section in *Pierre* that deals with Plinlimmon's essay tells us important things—considered from the point of view of its moral rather than its psychological nature. It is here that critical interpretation is divided. Some critics, for instance Yvor Winters in

68

Maule's Curse, see the "virtuous expediency" as the solution of Pierre's problem; however, Winters and critics of similar conviction appear to be victims of Pierre's rationalization in the same way that Pierre is a victim. As Henry Murray points out in his brilliant, hundred-page introduction to the 1949 Hendricks House edition of *Pierre,* the correlation of Pierre's role with chronometrical (Christ's) truth is a sophistry, another example of the "willed" creation of the central consciousness as he negates the outer world and makes his own, as if by magic. The complexity of *Pierre* rarely admits to a one-one ratio of character with projected metaphor, for the consciousness of Pierre himself so conditions the truth of the work that, though we can always question the depth of Melville's subtlety, we must accept the subtitle of the work—"The Ambiguities"—as a warning for the reader as well as, presumably, for Pierre.

But it is not the moral ambiguity of *Pierre* that concerns us here so much as the metaphysical ambiguity. The climate of a swollen, pretentious rhetoric at the beginning of the novel gives way—as nature gives way abruptly to the city—to the statement of nihilism that Pierre offers, partly to rationalize his passion for Isabel, partly as a judgment upon life. He says of Virtue and Vice: "a nothing is the substance, it casts one shadow one way, and another the other way; and these two shadows cast from one nothing; these, seems to me, are Virtue and Vice" (p. 382). Considered in the light of the latter part of the novel, the much-criticized rhetoric of the beginning is justified; it is the "nothing," the sickly, sweet, distorted pastoralism of nature and of human relationships that are to be investigated and found hollow. However, the distortion of nature and of relationships,

69

most specifically those of Pierre with his "sister"-mother, is not balanced by any countervision of a healthy nature; there is no alternate vision. Distortion gives way only to further distortion, so that the suspected "evil" of the city and its apparent metamorphosis in Pierre's cousin Glen Stanley is presented through a confused and hysterical prose, a kind of Dickensian or Shakespearean nightmare that is on the brink of becoming its own caricature.

But Pierre has already declared this world an illsuion. "It is all a dream—we dream that we dreamed we dream" (p. 383). And he goes on to say: "How can one sin in a dream?" Melville is asking here a profound question. How is it possible to commit sins, that is, acts of conscious will, in a world of illusions—the most terrifying of all illusions being the mastery of the self by the ego? The order of Saddle Meadows and of nature has disintegrated into a chaotic dream of solipsism, a fantasy in which the hero is divided against himself, raging against himself, over a matter that he has really forgotten and that was, in itself, never worth this ordeal. Pierre has said his "No," but he does not end in defiance: "Pierre is neuter now," he states. He does not belong to the infinite universe of the earlier novels. Like the symbolic Enceladus, he is "heaven-aspiring but still not wholly earth-emancipated"; he is, then, the pseudo-god who is, in a way that Ahab never is, slammed back to earth, to his own finite consciousness of himself. Just as nature is not her own interpreter, but a "cunning alphabet whereby . . . each man reads his own peculiar lesson . . . ," so is the apparent dualism between good and evil an illusion, a fantasy that must die with the imagination that could create and sustain it. So the "good" angel and the "bad" angel die along with Pierre, who was their creator

70

and measure; they do not survive him. Good and evil exist only in man, as confused (because simplified) abstractions.

Pierre has been considered in such detail because it marks the beginning of the apparent Timonism of *The Confidence-Man*, which is a continuation of the theme of *Pierre*; and it marks also, though the relationships may appear puzzling, the beginning of that climate of mind that can give us, without incongruity, the work *Billy Budd*. We see how in *Pierre* the dualism of the world is rejected, and the power of blackness, if there is any, is so ubiquitous as to dissolve into a meaningless generality. The "No, in thunder!" notion, if considered in relationship to Pierre, seems now inconclusive and misleading. The dramatic naysaying with which one is to confront the Devil becomes for Melville, in 1853, the turning-away of Bartleby to the wall with his knees drawn up, the final withdrawal from a world that was, to Bartleby, not violent but only a little cruel—but a world in which, nevertheless, he did not prefer to live. In this withdrawal it would be difficult to discover even a quiet heroism; the identification of the self-disqualification from life that Bartleby wills upon himself, and that is at the same time an obvious desire for death, with a somehow valuable gesture for the writer (as Leslie Fiedler suggests),[6] seems only puzzling.

This surface display of negation, and of a concern for a dualistic universe of irreconcilable forces, is dealt with in the next of Melville's novels, *The Confidence-Man*, written in 1857. Long unpopular because of its apparent pessimism and its wearying and often inconclusive narrative, *The Confidence-Man* is centrally flawed in that its "comedy of action" dissolves backward into a comedy of

71

speculation, to reverse Melville's stated intention. So the work, concerned with philosophical problems, does not always translate itself into art but remains conversation, vaguely dialectical, at its worst accumulative and concentric.

It will help to think of *The Confidence-Man* as a series of tales of a perhaps feigned Manichean dualism, about which the confidence-man dreams a long and complicated dream. The atmosphere of the dream, so much more strident than in *Pierre*, allows the confidence-man a certain omnipotence—the power of assuming and rejecting identity, or the various forms of his central identity; he is, then, in the unique position of an author. If the tales constitute a dream, at their core we find the atmosphere of a fallen world and the peculiar desire on the part of the protagonist to posit faith and test it, perhaps a secret desire for this faith to triumph: for surely if the confidence-man continually triumphs in his gulling of victims, it is Christianity that triumphs, paradoxically, because its innocence and charity cannot recognize hypocrisy ("only God can recognize a hypocrite"). When the confidence-man is defeated, Christianity itself is defeated, for it is no longer innocent. The loss of the confidence-man is a token of the hypocrisy of Christianity itself—like the life preserver examined in the concluding pages of the novel, it "looks so perfect—sounds so hollow." The confidence-man is the hero of this world, and the measure of his odd heroism is not his own confidence or cunning but rather the vulnerability of the world that he can easily seduce. The pattern of clashes of will and dialectical movement to a resolution (usually the confidence-man's victory) suggests a dualism, a representation of opposed forces. But an examination of the assumptions of the confidence-man will show that this surface dualism is but an appearance, and the underlying motif of the novel is not the tension of antipodal forces but rather the fact of no tension—of a final nihilism.

The surface dualism is suggested at the outset in the juxtaposition of the Christlike mute and the Negro beggar, and the doctrine of charity and the "no trust" world. To take the first figure as an antithesis to the guises of the confidence-man that follow would be to read the story on the level on which the dualism of the theological universe—in a sense Christian, but in a cruder sense Manichean—is taken as a legitimate struggle. The figure might also be seen as the ironic counterpart of the distrustful world which is preyed upon, a figure suggestive not only of the ironic incompatibility of earthly ethic and earthly practice—the Christian value of charity and the fact of individual materialism and national capitalism— but also of the basic incompatibility of this earthly ethic and the divine metaphysics in which it is presumably grounded. Here the "chronometrical and horological" antithesis would be a true metaphor, as it is not in *Pierre*. The figure of innocence, however, may also be interpreted as part of the masquerade itself, displaying the lulling platitudes that the confidence-man will subsequently exploit. But the most satisfying interpretation of the mute is to take him not as a character discrete from the action of the story, and not simply as the first of the confidence-man's guises, but rather as the symbolic representation in the mind of the dreamer (the authorlike central consciousness) of a heavenly ethic that is, indeed, to be proved unsuited for the world, and the purity of which will be rhetorically sustained as the ideal of Christian principle that, in its particularized forms, is to be tested and exposed.

It is the personality of the confidence-man in his role of testing this principle, and undergoing an education of his own, that unites the novel. The confidence-man cannot be understood except as the embodiment of an idea. He posits himself as the diabolical agent seeking to lure and betray an unsuspecting "good," and while it is certainly going too far to suggest that the confidence-man really represents Christian value in discord with a secular world, it is assuming too much to see him as an agent of the Devil—or the devil himself—as if this were the extent of the problem Melville sees. The confidence-man is in many ways less human than Milton's Satan, to whom he bears some resemblance, and he has none of the vicious sensuality that characterizes Chaucer's Pardoner, the *faux-semblant* of another pilgrimage. The confidence-man is a man—that is, human and finite—but he is not human in the sense in which these two characters are human, for it is precisely what is human that must be fiercely resisted. It is, finally, the avarice and sensuality of the Pardoner that disqualify him for real evil and, to a lesser extent, the undercutting recognition of the absurdity of his position that thwarts Milton's Satan. The Pardoner represents a complexity of character that does not need discussion here, but the frustration of his capacity for any real or ultimate evil is the result of his commitment to the human—for the forces of hell must be as little tempted by lust as by love. Melville surely had some aspects of Milton's Satan in mind, however, in creating his confidence-man: he is equated with the Devil "gulling Eve"; he is associated with snake imagery—he "writhes"; he exercises a hypnotic fascination upon his victims and, in an ironic reversal, he is suggested as the creature who charms man (as opposed to the usual snake-charming human being). But Milton's Satan recognizes a belief—however despised—in the Christian myth that the confidence-man would not be prepared to make. Satan is doomed to defeat within a vast hierarchical tautology, while the confidence-man's problem is more complicated, more resourceful, than the usual struggle between good and evil, between God and the Devil with the earth as the stage; at bottom it is a concern obsessed with the sheer burden of defining this struggle.

As the herb doctor, the professor of confidence says: " 'Granting that [dependence] on my medicine [is] in vain, is it kind to deprive him of what, in mere imagination, if nothing more, may help eke out, with hope, his disease?' " [7] At this point he is speaking to the Missouri bachelor about a third person, a sick man. The assumption is that the myth of charity, as it protects man against a reality too heartless to be borne, is to be valued for its illusory nature; the motif is one of a constant tension between truth—the pitiless ground base of nature's indifference and the "no trust" of the human heart—and the illusion of man's creation, which is confidence. The Missouri bachelor, who presents a skeptical counterpoint to the confidence-man, is later gulled; his cynicism is not so deep, nor so sophisticated, as that of the confidence-man. The education of the confidence-man himself, however, is only now to begin. In his guise as the cosmopolitan he says, " 'Life is a picnic *en costume*; one must take a part, assume a character, stand ready in a sensible way to play the fool' " (p. 161).

The confidence-man is obsessed with a desire to pene-

75

trate through the mask of humanity to the heart within.
The metaphor for this obsession, however diminished, is
the mysterious interlude of "Indian-hating." As measured against the whole of the novel, what is hated is not
the gullibility of the human heart—and not even its persistent eagerness to believe contrary to nature in the kind
of confidence the confidence-man so glibly advocates—
but rather in the condition of man himself, of the human
heart. The vengeance is necessarily a vengeance back
upon the self. Like most victimizers, in fiction at least,
the confidence-man is himself a victim; he has not the
vacuum of conscience, the lack of self-consciousness that
is the virtue of the true "Indian-hater." This Indian-hater
"commits himself to the forest primeval; there, so long as
life shall be his, to act upon a calm, cloistered scheme of
strategical, implacable, and lonesome vengeance" (p.
179). The Indian-hater works out his vengeance upon a
comparatively simple level. He does no more than isolate
his idea of depravity or evil into a segment of humanity,
and then attempt to exorcise this evil. He has a "devout
sentiment": he does not possess the ultimate cynicism of
the confidence-man; he has not the flashes of self-
consciousness that undercut the mission of another "Indian-hater," Captain Ahab. Ahab is much more complex: the white whale is never diminished by his hatred
but is instead given a meaning beyond itself. The In-
dians, however, are diminished out of their humanity by
the Indian-hater and, on the level of a personified abstraction, can be destroyed with righteousness. The confidence-man, however, cannot so simplify his role.

That his confidence is feigned is suggested all along
and revealed most obviously in the tale of the gentleman
madman, one of the many tales within the novel. The

confidence-man sees his consciousness of the condition of the human heart in relation to his external role of confidence *en costume* as the grave hidden by the flowers that are "made to bloom over it." This insight is expressed shortly afterward by the cynical transcendentalist disciple: " 'I will hear nothing of that fine babble about development and its laws; there is no development in the opinion and feeling but the developments of time and tide' " (p. 260). What is changeable is the human heart, and from this everything stems. Melville sees, as does Hawthorne in his conclusion to "Earth's Holocaust," "the heart, the heart—there was the little yet boundless sphere wherein existed the original wrong of which the crime and the misery of this outward world are merely types."

The education of the confidence-man progresses in proportion to the degree of complexity and cynicism expressed by the people he meets—though, since the novel does have the persistent atmosphere of a dream, one feels that the confidence-man already possesses whatever knowledge is revealed to him. The "cold prism" of the transcendental intellect is more than a match for the confidence-man's charm: he cannot defeat it; his professed faith in confidence is seen as a philosophy "contrary to the ways of the world . . . a cheat and a dream"; he himself is seen as the charmer who must expect to be victimized by those he charms. He is educated not to the truth of transcendentalism, or to its finer ethics, but rather to the essential cruelty and inhumanity, even the triteness, of the transcendental ethic when it has been enticed down to the level of the particular.

There is a fault in assuming that, given two apparently antithetical points of view, one must necessarily be right and the other wrong. Melville's intention is to display the hollowness, the inadequacy, of both points of view: the truth that will not be comforted, the "no trust" world, the grave beneath the flowers, the transcendental ethic, the discomforting reality that underlies appearance —and, against this, the world of professed Christianity, the faith in charity, in confidence. The confidence-man's defeat at the hands of the transcendentalist disciple is a token of the ultimate defeat of the surface confidence of the heart by the irrefragable reality that underlies it—the grave beneath. But the confidence that cannot be betrayed, that does not even exist, is more deadly than the instrument that would betray this confidence. Here there is no longer, to use Conrad's phrase, a "choice of nightmares." To read the novel as a working-out of the theme of the necessity of coming to terms with evil through a compromise of divine ethics and earthly necessity, as James E. Miller, Jr. suggests[8] (the "virtuous expediency" of *Pierre?*), is to accept the fallacy that there is a necessity beyond the tautological discipline of philosophical logic that truth must lie within one of two opposing points—that, given the confidence-man's deceit, the rationalism of the transcendentalist disciple is, then, what Melville condones. A compromise of what is divine and what is human in a mean of adaptation of divine law is not the struggle here: the struggle is rather one of the consciousness of the confidence-man that there is, perhaps, no real struggle at all, no polarity of "good and evil," "truth and falsity," and nothing to sustain the struggle through time. Both transcendentalism and the feigned confidence of the cosmopolitan are but the expression of the time's vast descendentalism of spirit that reduces even the consciousness of an intelligent irony to this sequence of cheap tricks. After his symbolic defeat by the transcendentalist, the confidence-man begins to move away from us. The final betrayal, the episode of the old man and the solar lamp, seems a parallel of the first chapter. The fantasy, coming to an end, is rawer, reveals more of itself; the persons involved, especially the boy who seems conjured up to test the old man's faith, seem little more than products of the confidence-man's imagination. The game itself has become hollow; there is no longer any contest. We have at the end not only a confidence-man who does not believe in confidence, but a Christian who does not believe in Christianity—who is, therefore, not a Christian. Confidence is, in a final irony, to be equated with God; the confidence-man says, "I believe in a Committee of Safety . . . in an invisible patrol. . . . In short . . . Jehovah shall be thy confidence." But the solar lamp, the symbol of truth, of confidence, of God, of the "conscience" in Father Mapple's sermon on Jonah, begins to dim. The final movement is a movement into darkness: it is not the triumph of evil over good but rather the negation of struggle, the disintegration into an underlying nihilism that has resulted, within the novel, from the long series of negations that constitute the confidence-man's experience. The daedal boat of the tale, the Fidele, speeds "as a dream." When Pierre asks how one can sin in a dream his question is predicated by a sense of the foundationless belief in ethics, in good or evil, or sin, that is sustained generally in his world and in the world of *The Confidence-Man* through the communion of superficial souls. It is important to see, though the

79

observation may appear odd, that for the force of evil as well as the force of good the struggle must be sustained, the disintegration into nihilism must be resisted. On the more immediate level, without confidence in man, in society, one falls into despair; and the condition of man is a shuttling movement between the illusory contentment of charity and the confrontation of the truth that will not be comforted—that is, despair. That the novel is a comedy, for all its bitterness, for even its final pessimism, is a token of the presumption involved in the attempt of man to penetrate the world of appearance—to believe in an ethic as well as create it, to formulate an ethical value of truth in a world in which, in the end, ethics can have no real foundation.

Lawrance Thompson believes that the essential element in Melville's thought is disappointing because "[it] narrows down to the sharp focus of a misanthropic notion that the world was put together wrong, and that God was to blame. He spent his life . . . sneering at God, accusing God . . . and (as he thought) quarreling with God. . . . Like his own Captain Ahab, he remained a defiant rebel, even in the face of death." [9] Thompson, to be true to his thesis, even to the title of his book, *Melville's Quarrel With God*, cannot go with Melville to the point of nihilism. To interpret *Billy Budd* as Thompson does, so that it makes sense in such an argument (that Melville is somehow "quarreling" with God), requires a certain distortion of the obvious mood of the story. It is far easier to read *Billy Budd* as Melville's final expression of acceptance, of a heroism in the face of injustice that is able, by its own will, to create justice. But the problem for a critic as well as for the general reader of *Billy Budd* may well lie in the reversal

80

of values that we commonly accept—the idea of conscious, historical, civilized life as a good, and the idea of death as an evil. Once the normal human assumption that death is evil is removed, Thompson's entire argument dissolves. In *Billy Budd*, the quest theme of Melville has run its course. We have no Adamic-turned-Faustian hero, a superman of sorts like Ahab, Pierre, and the confidence-man; we have instead individuals like Billy and Vere and Claggart, one-dimensional, almost passive role-takers in a triangle of archetypal scope.

The problem of *Billy Budd*, then, stems from the disintegration of the quest and from the acceptance of death as not evil—which leads romantically to the sailor's apotheosis in the folklore of his time, and classically to the acceptance of social necessity, of forms and order. But the intent of the work may well transcend this compatible dichotomy to suggest an acceptance of impending death, of annihilation, in somewhat Nirvanic terms, for the work is "angry," or represents part of a "quarrel" only if death is taken, as it conventionally is, to be at least painful and frightening. The terror of the white whale, infinity pressing back upon its perceiver (or creator), becomes here the transcendental dissolving of considerations of good and evil, of struggle, of life itself. Walter Sutton interprets *Billy Budd* in the light of Melville's interest in Buddhism and Schopenhauer, and sees the movement of the novel as a renunciation of the will that is the "highest consummation of life." [10] The Nirvanic quest has no faith in Buddha as a god, but only in Buddhism as an expression of negation. Thus the end of life—by extension, never to have lived—is the equivalent of the Christian's ascension and final communion with his God. So Vere does little to save Billy's life, and Billy's

last words—to be contrasted, surely, with the savage re-
belliousness of a White Jacket—are words of a positive
nature, perhaps of gratitude. The untouched innocence
of Billy, his pre-Adamic condition, is saved from the
world of experience that wounds Captain Vere; untouched, both are apotheosized and annihilated: "God
bless Captain Vere!" Billy says, and his words precede a
double death, that of Billy and Vere himself.

The experience of Vere is in broad terms that of the
father who manipulates the figure of innocence into the
transcendent Nirvana of nonexperience and nonidentity
that he himself will earn, after a time, but that he has
reached only after this experience—which invariably
wounds—in the painful world of appearances, of good
and evil, of constant struggle, and, most perniciously, of
unnatural, repressed lusts. For a writer whose aim is to
penetrate into a "basic truth," the sustainment of any two
points of view will suggest, in the end, the mockery of
assigning to one of two antithetical views a positiveness
worthy of one's faith—worthy of one's life. The quest
ends, ideally, in the negation and not in the compromise
or resolution of tension in Melville's irreconcilable world
of opposites; it is at once a transcendence and an annihilation, no longer an image of romantic diffusion as in
White Jacket, surely not an image of the vicious and self-
consuming pessimism of *Pierre*.

The intention of this essay has not been to examine
critically all facets of Melville's apparent drift into nihilism—this would involve, as well, as close study of Melville's reading of Schopenhauer—but rather to undercut
the general tone of simplicity in which Melville is often
discussed. The cliché of the "defiant rebel" represents
but an arresting of Melville's thought at a point fairly

early in his career; a study of Melville's movement away from this stance, as well as to it, is necessary to provide a fair view of the metaphysical and ethical implications of his work. Nineteenth-century in his conception of the forms of fiction and of "characterization," Melville is strikingly contemporary in his conception of the internal tensions that comprise a work. In a sense he is not a writer of "fiction" at all, but a writer of ideas who is using the means of fiction; let us speculate that he used fiction because of its essential ambiguity, its "muteness," and because of the possibility of his hiding behind its disguises. Just as he dares to do no more than hint at the homosexual perversion of sailors in *White Jacket* and *Billy Budd*, so, in mid- nineteenth-century America he can do no more than hint at the blankness behind the age-old negotiable forms of virtue and vice, good and evil, God and the Devil.

4

TRAGIC AND COMIC VISIONS IN "The Brothers Karamazov"

There is no writer who better demonstrates the contradictions and fluctuations of the creative mind than Dostoevski, and Dostoevski nowhere more astonishingly than in *The Brothers Karamazov*. Of the psychology of Dostoevski's works a great deal has been said—Nietzsche pronounced him the only psychologist from whom he learned anything—and of the ideas of *The Brothers Karamazov* much has been argued. In this essay I would like to discuss the various components of the novel—psychology, ideas, structure, fiction—only as they relate to the work as a creative act. For it is clear even upon a superficial first reading that this novel is like few other great works; it seems almost a novel in the making, a novel as it is being written, *in the very process of being imagined.*

Not that it is crudely improvised: like most of Dostoevski's novels, it is well planned, blocked out in a general pattern of point and counterpoint. The novel moves toward one clear statement about the transformation of suffering into joy, in preparation, as Dostoevski states in his preface, for the novel that is his real concern—a novel he did not live to write that was to be called *The Life of a Great Sinner.* The sadistic and disturbing novel we do have ends with the words, " 'Hurrah for Karamazov!' " The explicit novel—the daylight novel—is one of affirmation underscored not just by the juggling of sequences so that the young boys who are Alyosha's friends have the last word, but by the voice of the "narrator" throughout. Whenever the anonymous narrator speaks as a person, the novel sinks to a simplistic moral level that clearly seems the level Dostoevski wants, since he feels the necessity of bringing his novel back again and again to this level, no matter how far it has soared from it. When the narrator disappears, and the characters come alive—in long, rambling, and often hysterical speeches— the novel attains a vitality that wrenches its parts out of relationship to the whole. One can argue that this is also what the author "wants," but, if so, then this Dostoevski seems to be someone other than the author of the total work called *The Brothers Karamazov.* Structurally, the novel moves to a great trial scene, which is to try everyone, but this scene is the climax only of the external novel. The bewildering sense of incompleteness one feels after having read the novel is perhaps explained by the fact of the novel's being written (however it may have

88

been planned) with a double of itself contained in its most brilliant pages, a kind of shadow or antinovel whose tragedy mocks the positive accomplishments of the larger, Christian work. Two visions—one existential and tragic, the other Christian and "comic"—are unequally balanced in this novel and do not in my opinion resolve themselves.

Though most readers are familiar with the plot of *The Brothers Karamazov*, its very length and intricacy necessitate summary. One can see how Dostoevski has imagined his work structurally: a series of statements, the best of them dramatized, are worked out, qualified, or refuted by what follows them. Book 1 is called "The History of a Family," and here the narrator—surely Dostoevski's voice—reports on the history of the bizarre Karamazov family, stressing by his technique the epic and realistic mode and never the poetical and imaginative, for this is not fiction but rather *history*, and the Karamazovs *are* Russia. Dostoevski's style seems at first to be no style at all, but simply reporting. It is bare of all adornment, all fanciful description; nature is never imagined as the slightly distorted landscape viewed by man, but only as a stage backdrop against which man acts out his drama. There are no metaphors in Dostoevski's writing because his works as wholes are metaphors themselves.

Book 2, the "Unfortunate Gathering" in Father Zossima's cell, dramatizes the conflicts implicit in book 1. The gathering, which is Ivan's idea, is entirely improbable: Dostoevski brings together in this symbolic episode all significant characters and all significant philosophical conflicts, minor themes are introduced by implication, and the brothers Ivan and Mitya are confronted with the prophetic insight of Father Zossima. The fates of these two brothers are taken up in the next three books, "The Sensualists," in which Mitya explains his torment, and "Lacerations," in which the masochistic impulses of several characters, including Ivan, are dramatized, and "Pro and Contra." This book contains the famous "Grand Inquisitor" sequence, in which the complex and mysterious Ivan explains himself to his brother Alyosha. The anguish of rebellion against God's world can be seen to account for the various lacerations of the preceding books: something is wrong, something ruined in human nature, and Ivan is the only person articulate enough to explain it. Book 6, "The Russian Monk," is an answer to Ivan's questions, its very length and its repetitious piety addressed to the impatience of the young Ivan.

The conclusion of "The Russian Monk" contains Dostoevski's famous definition of hell as "the suffering of being unable to love"; it is clearly a diagnosis of the sorrows of the modern world. But book 7, "Alyosha," forces the reader (as it forces the young hero) into a realization of the mystery of the world and the futility of human wishes, in the rather grotesque episode in which the corpse of Father Zossima begins to decompose more rapidly than seems natural. Alyosha is then precipitated into the "world," represented by Grushenka, but is not conquered by it. The next two books deal with Mitya's drunken happiness and his arrest. Book 10, following, is a contrasting account of the relationships between boys of the village, the "new generation"; one of them is a young Ivan. Book 11, "Ivan," is in direct contrast to book 10, containing the interviews with the half brother, Smerdyakov, and the devil, who may or may not be Ivan's hallucination. Book 12 is the great trial scene, in which everyone is shown to be on trial, and the epilogue deals with the plans for Mitya's escape and the magical rebirth of joy and communion between Alyosha and the boys over the grave of the child Ilusha. Out of the novel's several deaths come this resurrection and an implied transformation of the "Karamazov" or Russian potentiality in the boys under Alyosha's influence. "How good life is when one does something good and just!" Alyosha exclaims.

The novel as it is summarized dramatizes the epigraph from the Book of John: "Verily, verily, I say unto you, except a corn of wheat fall into the ground and die, it abideth alone: but if it die, it bringeth forth much fruit." Every significant character in the novel—Mitya, Grushenka, Alyosha, Katerina, even Ivan—is transformed. Ivan's brain fever is symptomatic of his particular sin— the sin of intellectual pride. That he is perhaps mad is a way of pointing toward his future regeneration, though Dostoevski evidently did not feel that he could violate Ivan's character, as he did Raskolnikov's, in providing for a ritual conversion. The bulk of the novel is one of affirmation, though Ivan, the most eloquent person in the novel, is not saved but is made impotent, broken, most violently changed.

The problems of *The Brothers Karamazov* are not due to any weakness on the author's part, but to his extraordinary inventiveness. Within the confines of his careful structure a series of mocking antitheses appear: have they been created consciously or unconsciously? Are they ingenious, or are they simply mistakes? The key to Dostoevski's genius, however, seems to be in his command of the dynamics of fiction. Not life, certainly: life is never equal to the pace and intricacy of any of Dostoevski's works. The theme of transformation or rebirth is more than simply a religious (and rather magical) idea; it is a part of Dostoevski's imagination. Reality is constantly turning into something else; simplicity breaks up into fragments, baffling us; nothing stays, nothing is permanent; characters who are defined in one way break loose and assume deeper, vaster dimensions; dogmatic truths are echoed and mocked hundreds of pages later; the revered father figure is shadowed by demonic father figures; doubles multiply and question the very basis of individual identity; what is intended to be a parable or prophecy (Russian spirit threatened by European intellect) becomes a great mystic work in which all of men's acts, whether "good" or "evil," are held finally to be of little account, for it is precisely this heresy of Ivan's tragic pride, his assumption that man's sin is of importance, that Dostoevski wants to destroy.

The narrator of the novel seems at times to be speaking directly for the author; at other times he is refined out of individual existence, simply an omniscient point of view. He reveals himself in the trial scene (book 12) as "far from esteeming myself capable of reporting all that took place . . . I may have selected as of most interest what was of secondary importance. . . . But I see I shall do better not to apologize. I will do my best and the reader will see for himself that I have done all I can." Here, after eight hundred pages of the closest possible attention to his heroes' thoughts, the narrator "sees" them evidently for the first time and pronounces rather stern judgments upon them. Mitya and Grushenka made bad impressions; Alyosha is not particularly impressive. The novel begins with much attention paid to the old father, Fyodor Pavlovitch Karamazov: "a strange type

. . . abject and vicious and at the same time senseless."
He is seen to be rather naive and simple: "As a general
rule, people, even the wicked, are much more naive and
simple-hearted than we suppose. And we ourselves are,
too."

When Dostoevski begins to consider Fyodor seriously,
however, the old man's character changes. We witness in
his speeches the very genesis and development of a fictional creation. The perverse buffoonery of the lecherous
old man turns into a shrewd, sinister, even diabolic wit
when he begins to talk:

> "So you want to be a monk? . . . Well, it's a good op-
> portunity. You'll pray for us sinners; we have sinned too much
> here. I've always been thinking who would pray for me. . . .
> You see, however stupid I am about it, I keep thinking, I keep
> thinking—from time to time, of course, not all the while.
> It's impossible, I think, for the devils to forget to drag me
> down to hell with their hooks when I die. Then I wonder—
> hooks? Where would they get them? What of? Iron hooks?
> . . . Now I'm ready to believe in hell, but without a ceiling.
> It makes it more refined, more enlightened. . . . And, after
> all, what does it matter whether it has a ceiling or hasn't?
> But, do you know, there's a damnable question involved in it?
> If there's no ceiling there can be no hooks, and if there are
> no hooks it all breaks down, which is unlikely again, for then
> there would be none to drag me down to hell, and if they
> don't drag me down what justice is there in the world? *Il fau-
> drait les inventer*, those hooks, on purpose for me alone."
> (p. 23)[1]

Though one would know that this is Dostoevskian, the
speech is uniquely Fyodor's; he is set off from Dostoevski's other buffoons by a certain perverse blend of the degraded and the spiritual, a brilliant comic creation who

93

cannot sit down to drink without questioning the meaning of life. He is filled with life, the base drive of the Karamazovs for life, and he springs into being for us time and again, opening to question the narrator's flat statements about him. There is something wonderful in so dedicated a baseness, one thinks; only Fyodor, bleeding from having been kicked in the face by Mitya, could forget his pain and become transported with lustful thoughts of Grushenka once he believes she is in the house. The most atrocious behavior in Father Zossima's cell is certainly Fyodor's; he has the audacity, or perhaps the insight, to ask Father Zossima, "Is there room for my humility beside your pride?" In the richness of Dostoevski's narration, nothing ever fulfills itself. Therefore, it ceases to develop, and is immediately transformed into something else. Characters are introduced, summarized, and, when they come to life, display remarkable complexities that were certainly not imagined in Dostoevski's exposition—but only in his drama. And though the most audacious behavior is old Fyodor's, the cruellest behavior is Ivan's. In striking the foolish Maximov and knocking him from the carriage, Ivan commits the only act of violence up until this point, astonishing his father with his brutality.

The other remarkable metamorphosis of character takes place in Smerdyakov. The fourth son, the shadowy illegitimate child of Fyodor's lust, Smerdyakov is a warning that man's sins will come back to him; the sins of old Russia will destroy her and out of this violence a new Russia will be born. Smerdyakov, imagined intially as a kind of idiot, an epileptic "chicken" who has no courage, no intelligence, and who is capable only of echoing Ivan's radical ideas, emerges as superior even to Ivan; he is the killer of their father, Ivan's "instrument," but at all times shrewder and more perceptive than Ivan himself. As Ivan's "shadow" he acts out Ivan's suppressed or un-realized wish, which is recognizable as the act of a Dostoevskian double, but the creation of Smerdyakov himself is an extraordinary one. The fact that Smerdyakov, like the author, is an epileptic, the fact that the sickish, affected, pompous young man emerges as one of the strongest characters in the novel, supports Freud's observation of the role of the criminal in Dostoevski. Though Freud ignores Ivan's relationship to Smerdyakov and concentrates instead upon Mitya's (Freud is concerned with the sexual rivalry of father and son), what he says about the criminal is highly significant: the criminal to Dostoevski is almost a redeemer.[2] This is a startling reversal of Zossima's teachings—or perhaps a startling new view of them—for while Zossima instructs us to judge no one, to withhold condemning the criminal out of a feeling of Christian love for him, Freud suggests that the criminal himself is the blessed one, precisely because he commits the forbidden sin and thereby absolves us of our own desires for crime.

One must be grateful to the murderer, according to Freud, for, except for him, one would have been obliged to murder. Not kindly pity but rather the "identification on the basis of similar murderous impulses—in fact, a slightly displaced narcissism"—lies behind Dostoevski's insistence upon forgiving sin. And one notices with surprise how readily sin is forgiven in these novels. To kill with one's brain is evil, but to kill with one's passions is excusable; Ilusha's death, the result of Mitya's brutality, is simply an event on the way to Mitya's spiritual transformation!

95

The gradual development of Smerdyakov as a person, the shadowy brother emerging out of the darkness to control all destinies, is explicable in such terms if we understand that for Dostoevski the criminal is the true saint, one who sacrifices himself for the wishes of the community (note the insight of Lise and Ivan, who accuse the townspeople of liking the murder) and who must ultimately sacrifice himself. Zossima has preached sympathy for the suicides, who are the most unhappy of all. Smerdyakov's suicide is a parallel to Svidrigaïlov's; like Svidrigaïlov, the shadow-hero of *Crime and Punishment*, the true redeemer of that novel, Smerdyakov chooses death not because he despairs but because, having committed the act the novel has prepared him for, he no longer has any identity. All of Dostoevski's novels deal with the long preparation for the consummation of a violent act, without which the works could not be imagined. Though it would be difficult to prove, it seems likely that the acts of violence—the sheer consummation of murderous impulses designed to "change one's life"— are the bases upon which the novels were written; the ideological dialogues come second. Hence, the strange sympathy Dostoevski shows for his murderers, out of proportion to their behavior before or after their crimes; their boundless egoism is clearly no sin to him so long as it is not "rational." (It is interesting to note that the only despised and unforgiven characters in *The Brothers Karamazov* and *Crime and Punishment* are the mediocre, calculating, would-be liberals, Rakitin and Luzhin.) All this is suppressed or disguised in the narrator's voice, who withdraws from a discussion of Smerdyakov because this bastard son of Fyodor's is so insignificant: "I ought to say something of this Smerdyakov, but I am ashamed of keeping my readers' attention so long occupied with these common menials" (p. 118). It would seem that Dostoevski at this point has not clearly worked out the complex Smerdyakov of six hundred pages later; that Smerdyakov is a result of the creation of the novel itself, the fulfillment of a desire not immediately felt that the criminal not be a simple lackey but an intelligent man equal to the role of redeemer.

Of the use of "doubles" in Dostoevski much has been written. The literary "double" is a manifestation of the wish that, in a dream, would create itself as a concrete image. The dream-work is like the texture of formal allegory, personifications and desires being present as pictorial realities. In literature the double is a result of the author's conscious or unconscious desire for a wider range of action, possibilities of behavior for his hero that go beyond the morally acceptable, and this wish will create itself in the form of a double, or antihero. Dostoevski's second novel, *The Double*, explores the disintegrating ego of a schizophrenic as his other self emerges out of the darkness to claim his total identity. Such obvious works as *Moby Dick* and *Heart of Darkness* provide us with conventionally intelligent and moral narrators who are obsessed by the dark, satanic, murderous, and damned heroes at the center of their narratives, heroes who provide an important initiation and education for the observer—and they are clearly redeemers, also, dying with their forbidden knowledge available to the more ordinary observer (and the reader) who need not travel so far into the heart of darkness to realize such truth for himself. Handled skillfully, the story of the hero and his double makes the most satisfactory kind of narrative, for the

97

"hero" makes such claims upon the audience's loyalty that to allow him the range of all desire—which belongs to the shadow-hero, the antihero—would be unpleasant. Certain contemporary works, in refusing to grant readers the conventional moral protection provided by the double (for instance, Mailer's *An American Dream*) upset our sensibilities; we want the release of a consummation of violence, but we are frightened at having it offered so bluntly to us, the spectacle of an untrammeled ego being too close to our own fantasies for comfort.

Dostoevski's imagination is such that he conceives the kernel of his drama as a conflict within the parts of one self. We may assume that this self is Dostoevski. Lesser characters—for instance, Ilusha's father, Lise, Madame Hohlakov—are exaggerations, usually approaching caricature, of certain main obsessions. Critics have remarked upon the airlessness of Dostoevski's world, its failure to imagine nature as anything but a metaphorical Mother Earth existing only to be kissed, and clearly Dostoevski is concerned only with psychological drama. "One reptile will devour another," Ivan prophesizes grimly, and the irony—which he does not know—is that to have so perceptive an insight into the workings of this world will necessitate his being "devoured" as well. Dostoevski always punishes those characters who express what he is doing, the characters we feel are the closest to him—not only Smerdyakov and Svidrigaïlov, but also Stavrogin of *The Possessed.*

These doubles, imagined fantastically, exert influences upon one another that cannot be explained in any naturalistic way. There are moments of doubleness, of understanding and insight that must be denied (one always

98

denies the double), and there are peculiar echoings of ideas, ideas doubled and tripled as the novel proceeds. It is not just in the sequence involving Ivan and his devil that the question of individual identity comes up; the boundaries of one soul and the influence of wishes thought to be unvoiced are questioned throughout the novel, and in extraordinarily flat, banal prose. For instance, the relationship between Ivan and Smerdyakov is an obvious example of the relationship between mysterious doubles, with Ivan apparently the stronger and more intelligent, and Smerdyakov the instrument of his will. Ivan's unconscious wishes for his father's death direct Smerdyakov, who communicates with the unconscious directly; Smerdyakov is, then, the master, the controller of fate simply because he is able to penetrate the barrier of consciousness that must conventionally deny evil impulses.

Smerdyakov is linked explicitly to Ivan when he says to Aloshya that he knows nothing about Mitya: "It's not as if I were his keeper" (p. 269). Only a few pages later Ivan says, in answer to another question of Alyosha's about their brother, " 'You are always harping upon it! What have I to do with it? Am I my brother Dmitri's keeper?' " (p. 275) And there is a peculiar scene in "The Sensualists," in which old Fyodor, reminiscing drunkenly upon the exquisite tortures to which he subjected Alyosha's mother, is suddenly told by Ivan that this woman was his mother, too. The father says:

"Your mother? . . . What do you mean? What mother are you talking about? Was she? . . . Why, damn it! of course she was yours too! . . . Excuse me, why, I was thinking Ivan . . . He, he, he!" He stopped. A broad, drunken, half senseless grin overspread his face. (p. 164)

The father is either thinking that Ivan had no mother, being inhuman, or that he is the son of Lizaveta and, therefore, is identical with Smerdyakov. They are both the same age, twenty-four, and are momentarily confused in their father's mind. Alyosha, as well as Smerdyakov, functions as a kind of double for Ivan, though only from time to time. Alyosha's mysticism perhaps accounts for his being able to speak so directly to Ivan, past the defenses of Ivan's consciousness: "I only know one thing . . . it wasn't you killed father" (p. 732). Ivan is enraged by this declaration, but when Smerdyakov repeats it some pages later—"Why are your fingers [trembling] like that? Go home, you did not murder him" (p. 757) —he falters and is about to lose control of himself.

When Smerdyakov finally makes his contemptuous confession to Ivan, we have a typical Dostoevskian scene in which Smerdyakov takes off his garter and reaches unaccountably into his stocking:

"He's mad!" [Ivan] cried, and, rapidly jumping up, he drew back, so that he knocked his back against the wall and stood up against it, stiff and straight. He looked with insane terror at Smerdyakov, who, entirely unaffected by his terror, continued fumbling in his stocking, as though he were making an effort to get hold of something. (p. 759)

Typically Dostoevskian because it is bizarre and darkly comic, the scene is typical also because it demonstrates the awakening of the consciousness to the grotesque depths of the unconscious—the fumbling for and revelation of the truth, the suppressed wish. Such revelation pushes the coldly rational Ivan to "insane terror."

It is not only characters who are doubled; there is also a strange interweaving of ideas and attitudes in this novel, so that a tragic Zossima is parodied by the society lady, Madame Hohlakov. Ivan's refusal to acknowledge Christian love except as a form of self-laceration is anticipated by the shallow doubts of this society lady when she says:

"You see, I so love humanity that—would you believe it? —I often dream of forsaking all that I have, leaving Lise, and becoming a sister of mercy. . . . But could I endure such a life for long? . . . And, do you know, I came with horror to the conclusion that, if anything could dissipate my love to humanity, it would be ingratitude." (p. 63)

Father Zossima's statement about the impossibility of judging criminals, certainly meant to be serious—"no one can judge a criminal, until he recognizes that he is just such a criminal as the man standing before him" (p. 385)—is mercilessly parodied by this same woman some three hundred pages later:

"Let them acquit [Mitya]—that's so humane, and would show what a blessing reformed law courts are. . . . And if he is acquitted, make him come straight from the law courts to dinner with me, and I'll have a party of friends, and we'll drink to the reformed law courts. I don't believe he'd be dangerous; besides, I'll invite a great many friends, so that he could always be led out if he did anything. And then he might be made a justice of the peace or something in another town, for those who have been in trouble themselves make the best judges. And, besides, who isn't suffering from aberration nowadays?" (p. 703)

Dostoevski is at his best when he is being destructive. The cruellest doubling in the novel is the parallel implied between Ivan and the ignorant Father Ferapont. Ivan, disintegrating in the courtroom, talks of the devil's presence—"under that table with the material evidence on it, perhaps"—and reminds us suddenly of the religious fanaticism of the old monk, who sees devils everywhere; they have become in Father Zossima's time "as common as spiders in the corners" (p. 403).

The most interesting doubling is in relationship to the figure of the "father" in this novel. Alyosha's physical father, old Fyodor, is paralleled by Alyosha's spiritual father, Zossima; Zossima is paralleled by Ivan's Grand Inquisitor; the tragic nihilism of the Grand Inquisitor is, in turn, parodied by Ivan's devil, the "true" devil—shabby, second-rate, a buffoon who threatens to bring us back full circle to the father-as-buffoon, another version of Fyodor. What is stated by Father Zossima is questioned indirectly by the Grand Inquisitor, and the high seriousness of both is further questioned by the shabby devil. For instance, it is stated in the first book that Alyosha had unquestioning faith in the miraculous power of his elder:

Alyosha did not wonder why they loved him so, why they fell down before him and wept with emotion merely at seeing his face. Oh! he understood that for the humble soul of the Russian peasant, worn out by grief and toil, and still more by the everlasting injustice and . . . sin . . . it was the greatest need and comfort to find someone or something holy to fall down before and worship.

"Among us there is sin, injustice, and temptation, but yet, somewhere on earth there is someone holy and exalted. He has the truth; he knows the truth; so it is not dead upon the earth; so it will come one day to us, too, and rule over all the earth according to the promise." (p. 30)

This mystical faith in a kind of apocalyptic truth on its way to sinful mankind is always taken seriously by Dostoevski, who mixes it in his prophesizing with the future of Mother Russia. Surely Ivan's article on the dissolving of the State into the Church is a serious statement— though Ivan has written the article as a kind of jest, for, outside the Church, the criminal cannot be saved and will fall into despair. One comes back again and again to the criminal, who is the most important person because he alone of all people acts; he alone, by causing others to suffer and by passing through suffering himself, makes happiness possible.

But this mysticism, so fervently preached by Father Zossima, is given a different interpretation by Ivan's Grand Inquisitor. The Grand Inquisitor's secret is that he does not believe in God, but he is a victim of a terrible love for mankind. His indictment of Christ is that Christ himself does not love man and does not understand him; Christ, in refusing to display his powers through miracle, excludes from the State-as-Church most of humanity:

"Thou didst promise them the bread of Heaven, but, I repeat again, can it compare with earthly bread in the eyes of the weak, ever sinful and ignoble race of man? . . . what is to become of the millions . . . who will not have the strength to forego the earthly bread for the sake of the heavenly? Or dost thou care only for the . . . great and strong . . . ? No, we care for the weak too. They are sinful and rebellious, but in the end they too will become obedient. They will marvel at us and look on us as gods, because we are ready to endure the freedom which they have found so dreadful and to rule over them. . . . Choosing 'bread,' Thou wouldst have satisfied the universal and everlasting craving of humanity—to find someone to worship. So long as man remains free he strives for nothing so incessantly and so painfully as to find someone to worship." (p. 300-301)

In saying this, the Grand Inquisitor does not declare himself a foe of Father Zossima. On the contrary, they are identical; they are the same person, viewed by differing temperaments. Zossima is the mystic, and his mysticism has the psychological power of ridding the peasant (most of humanity) of his burden of freedom; the Grand Inquisitor is the mystic-turned-political figure, the organizer and savior of mankind. Both Zossima and the Grand Inquisitor are altruistic, ruled by love of man. Dostoevski presents these two passages with equal enthusiasm—one is not necessarily a parody or a demonic echo of the other. One points toward a cessation of individual anguish that is religious and "comic" in the sense in which the *Divine Comedy* is comic; the other is bitter in its assumption of the tragic role certain enlightened men must play on earth.

Like other religious conservatives, Dostoevski displays an anxiety over ridding the mind completely of any power over religion. If man's rationality is not to be allowed the possible destruction of religion through skepticism, it must be denied as well the possibility of belief. This is an extraordinary demand. Dostoevski's narrator says:

Oh! no doubt, in the monastery [Alyosha] fully believed in miracles, but, to my thinking, miracles are never a stumbling-block to the realist. It is not miracles that dispose realists to belief. The genuine realist, if he is an unbeliever, will always find strength and ability to disbelieve in the miraculous, and if he is confronted with a miracle as an irrefutable fact he would rather disbelieve his own senses than admit the fact. . . . Faith does not, in the realist, spring from the miracle but the miracle from faith. If the realist once believes, then he is bound by his very realism to admit the miraculous also.

104

The Apostle Thomas said that he would not believe till he saw, but when he did see he said, "My Lord and my God!" . . . he believed solely because he desired to believe. (p. 25)

Ivan's devil, in an ingenious attempt to make Ivan believe in his existence independent of Ivan's mind, echoes this:

"Don't believe it then. . . . what's the good of believing against your will? Besides, proofs are no help to believing, especially material proofs. Thomas believed, not because he saw Christ risen, but because he wanted to believe, before he saw." (p. 774)

These remarks, one offered by the narrator and the other by the "father of lies," support each other, though in a sense they exist in no relationship to each other at all. Both are perhaps "true" because they are truths of different worlds, different dimensions.

It is the incongruity of different dimensions brought together as if by magic that gives this novel its complex, richly varied texture. For instance, the thematic climax of the novel consists of Ivan's questions concerning the presence of evil and Father Zossima's answer to him. But even this central problem cannot be resolved, for we have a diabolical echoing of what should have been the final word: indeed, in Dostoevski there is no final word! Ivan, in "Pro and Contra," talks to Alyosha of the suffering of children, which seems to him entirely unjustified. His attack upon man's sadism is only a means to attacking God, who has allowed such horrors:

"Do you understand why this infamy must be and is permitted? Without it, I am told, man could not have existed on earth, for he could not have known good and evil. Why should he know that diabolical good and evil when it costs so much? Why, the whole world of knowledge is not worth that child's prayer to 'dear, kind God'!" (p. 287)

Ivan goes on to tell the story of the Russian landowner who has a child torn apart by hunting dogs, and asks if the man deserves "to be shot for the satisfaction of our moral feelings." But Ivan does not care for revenge, for a hell for oppressors. He wants to be able to forgive, but he cannot forgive; out of a love for humanity he will not accept the "harmony" that is based upon suffering and forgiveness. "I would rather be left with the unavenged suffering. I would rather remain with my unavenged suffering and unsatisfied indignation, *even if I were wrong*": this must be the first statement of tragic existentialism ever written. There is a certain terror in the readiness to forgive, Ivan recognizes, and in so doing he strikes at the very basis of Dostoevski's sympathy for the criminal. What is this sympathy but a recognition of similar murderous impulses in the self?

It is not simply that Ivan represents the "intellectual" or the "European" in this novel; in a crucial way he represents the forbidden knowledge that lies in Dostoevski and in the religious temperament, a kind of spiritual sadism. No wonder, then, that Ivan will have to be destroyed. There has been a great deal of misleading criticism written about Ivan's place in this novel, particularly since the apparent orthodoxy of the work attracts critics of a conservative or reactionary nature. Here is Eliso Vivas on Ivan's predicament: "Thus it turns out that Ivan, who believes in the primacy of evil, when you press him, does not know, is an absolute solipsist, and cannot discover proof of the world, of God, or even of Satan.[3] And [Zossima's answer] resolves the conflict because it reveals that hell is life without love. And it also reveals that Ivan's dossier is possible only through a lie. For Ivan forgets that he is a creature, that he therefore has no right to challenge God." [4]

It would probably be pointless to suggest to Vivas that the whole idea of Ivan's suffering turns upon his "not knowing" and that his Euclidian earthly mind, being all he has, is all he will accept. In adhering to his instincts "even if he is wrong," Ivan is being true to the earth and is not betraying humanity. And who can "discover proof of the world, of God, or even of Satan"? Dostoevski argues constantly that one cannot "discover proof" of anything; the very idea of proof is repugnant to him. To say that Ivan forgets that he is a "creature" is to utter the most pathetic sort of nonsense. The existentialist accepts all responsibility for his actions and does not beg forgiveness, but he accepts absolutely no responsibility for actions that are not his own. The essentialist (in this context, the ideal Christian) accepts all guilt for all actions, is morally ubiquitous, has no singular identity, and can be forgiven for any sin, no matter how terrible, because he ultimately has no freedom and no responsibility, not simply for his own sins but for the sins of mankind; he is a "creature." To recognize oneself as a "creature" is, then, to submit gratefully to the condition of having no responsibility for one's actions—like Mitya, whose brutality transforms him and, incidentally, destroys others—and to remain forever a child. A critic like Vivas might be quite right, within his religious context, to disapprove of Hamlet's despair and recommend for him fasting and prayer—but this would not show much insight into the tragic vision of life, which is certainly opposed to the Christian vision.

Dostoevski understands perfectly the significance of Ivan's questions, and the answer he suggests for them is not so much an answer as another point of view. This is Zossima speaking on the Book of Job:

"I heard the words of mockery and blame, proud words, 'How could God give up the most loved of His saints for the diversion of the devil . . . and for no object except to boast to the devil?' . . . But the greatness of it lies just in the fact that it is a mystery." (p. 347–348)

"Mystery," then, is offered as a reasonable answer to Ivan's question, just as it is offered as a political expedient by the Grand Inquisitor. And Father Zossima goes on to say of the Bible:

"And what mysteries are solved and reveal; God raises Job again, gives him wealth again. Many years pass by, and he has other children and loves them. But how could he love those new ones when those first children are no more? . . . Remembering them, how could he be fully happy? . . . But he could, he could. It's the great mystery of human life that old grief passes gradually into quiet tender joy." (p. 348)

Dostoevski offers here no "answer" to Ivan's demands, and certainly the existential mind is offended at the ease with which pain is righted through words; the children who suffer and die clearly do not exist for Father Zossima as existing individuals, but only as objects in a continuous evolution that brings us closer to God and "truth." If there is to be punishment for deeds of evil, it will have to be self-punishment. Zossima teaches that one cannot judge the criminal, but he says:

"If you can take upon yourself the crime of the criminal your heart is judging, take it at once, suffer for him . . . and let him go without reproach. . . . If, after your kiss, he goes away untouched, mocking at you, do not let that be a stumbling-block. . . . It shows his time has not yet come. . . . And if it come not, no matter; if not he, then another in his place will understand and suffer, and judge and condemn himself, and the truth will be fulfilled." (p. 385)

In such Christianity, then, it is precisely the individual who does not exist. One individual or another, one grasp of truth or another, it does not matter: truth itself is all that matters. So Zossima's religion is the same religion as that of the Grand Inquisitor: the existing individual is of no importance. One needs "saints" to bow down to, but it is the bowing down that is significant, not the fact that a certain individual bows down. Dostoevski imagines the Grand Inquisitor as the pragmatic representative of Zossima's mysticism. Both are lovers of mankind, but the Grand Inquisitor, in rejecting God, realizes that all men need laws and punishments and the process of confession and absolution. But both the Grand Inquisitor and Father Zossima recognize that man is a child—he is far from the existentialist's ideal of a fully committed, rational, responsible human being.

Then, having set up daytime and nighttime equivalents of saviors, Dostoevski cannot resist going further and hypothesizing a bitter antithesis to both. The arena is once again Ivan's mind, at the beginning of the illness brought on by Smerdyakov's confession. The devil who appears to him is a disappointment—a kind of poor relation addicted to French phrases (anything French is decadent to Dostoevski) and strained jokes, the very bottom of Ivan's unconscious powers and therefore the most frustrating of his trials; he is a blow to Ivan's pride, like the dwarfish devil who rides Nietzsche's Zarathustra and the "flabby devil" of Conrad's *Heart of Darkness*. What this devil is, of course, is the human mind, and out of it everything has come. That Dostoevski knows this seems clear enough, though he will pass beyond it in creating his epic comedy of faith. The devil says:

"*Je pense, donc je suis,* I know that for a fact, all the rest, all these worlds, God and even Satan—all that is not proved, to my mind. Does all that exist of itself, or is it only an emanation of myself, a logical development of my ego which alone has existed forever?" (p. 781)

He echoes Ivan's earlier remarks in saying that life is possible only by virtue of the absurd; without the scapegoat of the devil (or man's unpredictable mind) nothing would have come to pass. The "devil" is equated with the "irrational":

"For all their indisputable intelligence, men take this farce as something serious, and that is their tragedy. They suffer, of course . . . but then they live, they live a real life, not a fantastic one, for suffering is life." (p. 780)

Dostoevski says in this way that the basis of life is the irrational, the "devil" in man that mocks all too casually the farce of suffering that is human destiny. Of the Atonement nothing is said; this too is perhaps no more than an "emanation" from the mind of man.

But the harshest blow to the idealistic beliefs of Father Zossima is the devil's conception of conscience. What Dostoevski says here is absolutely in contradiction to what he has said earlier. Asked by Ivan about the tortures of hell, the devil says:

"What tortures? Ah, don't ask. In old days we had all sorts, but now they have taken chiefly to moral punishments —'the stings of conscience' and all that nonsense. . . . And

who's the better for it? Only those who have got no conscience, for how can they be tortured by conscience when
they have none?" (p. 782)

That Ivan is driven mad is no necessary indication that
his experience has been illusory; on the contrary, madness is often a sign in literature that the truth has blasted
away all normality. Like Pip of *Moby Dick*, like Hamlet
who plays mad and then no longer needs to play, Ivan
has realized something so devastating that he cannot
return to the world of ordinary men. He disappears from
the novel, lost in the bustle of preparing for the freedom
of Mitya and the "new Russia" symbolized by the boys.
"Men take this farce as something serious, and that is
their tragedy": Ivan's part in the novel is that of tragic
protagonist, making a certain choice (leaving his father
to be killed), overreaching in his estimation of his own
strength to bear the kind of truth he demands, and falling at last, destroyed by the fate that is so much a part of
his character as to be inseparable from him. His tragedy
differs significantly from that of Stavrogin in *The Possessed*, for Stavrogin lacks all will, all generosity, all purpose. As he says at the end of his life: "The only thing
that has come out of me is negation without strength.
. . . I can never lose my reason and never believe in an
idea the way [Kirilov] did. I cannot even get very deeply
interested in an idea." Indeed, Dostoevski is careful to
insist that Stavrogin is sane when he commits suicide—
remaining sane, resisting the grace of insanity, is symptomatic of Stavrogin's damnation. Though Ivan shares
some of Stavrogin's beliefs, he is far closer to humanity.
If Ivan is presented as the rational existentialist, then the
fate of such an intellectual and ethical position is madness and destruction, and such fate constitutes tragedy.

111

For we see that only those without consciences will survive and only the sensitive will suffer. The devil's glib
complaint about the new punishments is an answer to
Father Zossima, undercutting the elder's mystic conception of a man as a child thirsting for punishment and
forgiveness. On the contrary, to be a child is to be a
brute, and those few men who raise themselves above the
brute level will suffer and be destroyed.

One is driven, then, again and again to a reassessment
of this novel: is it an affirmative work, a kind of divine
comedy that successfully answers the questions it asks?
Or does it mock its very intentions, containing within it
an antinovel, a tragic vision of life that bitterly opposes
the joy of the ending? Kafka asks whether eternity can
wipe out the humiliation of time, and one answers such a
question in one of two ways: from the essentialist point of
view, in which eternity does indeed lose everything in it,
or from the existentialist point of view, in which there is
no eternity but only segments of time that are never
transcended. Dostoevski allows for both answers, though
he clearly intends the essentialist view to justify the
novel's sufferings. He is credited with a shrewd understanding of society and of human character, but in reality
he limits himself severely—probably by choice—in his
dealings with "society," and his characters all seem to belong to the same family; his psychological insights deal
mainly with the self-lacerating effects of egoism and its
corollary, the wish for destruction and death. As a writer
of ideas he is always fascinating until he brings his works
to a close. (Only *The Idiot*, with its beautifully shaped
form, and the bizarre *The Possessed*, with its unleashing
of Peter Verkhovensky onto the world, seem satisfactory

as wholes.) What has made Dostoevski so highly esteemed a writer is, perhaps, not his understanding of human nature or his ability to work intelligently with ideas, but rather his fluid demonstration of the art of writing—the splendid unpredictability of the writer as writer, who can *leave nothing unsaid*, whose imagination is so nervously rich that characters and ideas multiply themselves as if by their own volition. The highest vision that Dostoevski gives us is the vision of the unfathomable raw process of creation as it leaps from the unconscious.

5

CHEKHOV
and the Theater
of the Absurd

The faithful rendering of life as it is truly lived, its tragedy always conditioned by the relentless banality of life and so transformed into something akin to comedy; the insistence upon the unheroic, the unmelodramatic, the self-deceiving, the futile; the paralysis of will that is at once a mark of the cultured and a sign of their decadence: these are the obvious characteristics of Chekhov's drama. The point at which Chekhov's meticulous symbolic naturalism touches the inexplicable, the ludicrous, and the paradoxical is the point at which his relationship to our contemporary theater of the absurd is most clear. Much of what seems stunning and *avant garde* in the last

117

two decades of theater has been anticipated in both theory and practice by Chekhov. For instance, one has only to examine the central issues of *The Cherry Orchard* and *The Three Sisters*—the hopeless, comic-pathetic loss of a tradition and the futile longing for Moscow—to see how closely Chekhov is echoed in Beckett's *Waiting for Godot* and other works.

The concept of the "absurd" must be defined. It is a confusing term, for we are accustomed to equating the works of many modern writers with the existential concept of "absurdity." Sartre and Camus systematically examine the bases and the consequences of an absurd world, a world without meaning, but their works of literature, particularly their plays, are traditional in structure and language. However, when the playwright attempts to give expression to the absurd through both the structure and language of his work, he is then considered a playwright in the theater of the absurd (a term that could be set off by quotation marks, since its meaning is by no means simple). Chekhov's philosophical basis is clearly nineteenth-century naturalism, but his technique is only apparently naturalistic: it is fundamentally symbolic. What is absurd in Chekhov is the content of his works—what actually happens—and several of the devices he uses, particularly those dealing with language. Again and again we are confronted with intelligent people who have somehow lost their capacity for self-expression, whether wealthy landowners and their offspring, or working-class people, or the "emancipated." And with this capacity for self-expression they have also lost their ability to live.

All literature deals with contests of will, but drama makes most clear the spiritual struggles that life demands through its ritualistic enactment of the agon. Lifelong conflicts—conflicts of an abstract and spiritual nature—are given body, compressed, and played out before us on the stage. On the stage someone is either being born or dying; if his struggle is not with the resisting forces of other people (as in much of Shakespeare), it is with the forces of his unknown self, or, as in the Ionesco play *Exit the King*, with the force of death. Chekhov's works are tragedies of the impotence of will about to transform themselves into comedies, because their protagonists are diminished human beings; as Chekhov says, *The Cherry Orchard* is almost farcical in places,[1] though it deals with the end of an entire social order and the splitting-up of a family. This kind of bitter comedy is, perhaps, tragedy that can no longer sustain faith in itself.

In his philosophical grasp of his material, as well as in a number of particular dramatic devices, Chekhov anticipates the contemporary theater of the absurd. This essay will analyze the relationship between the techniques of Chekhov and the absurdist playwrights, mainly the distortions of dramatic and linguistic convention, the use of inexplicable incident and "arbitrary issue" or private poetic image, and the relentless rhythm of disintegration that pierces exteriors but deliberately fails to achieve a recognition of a solid underlying reality.

In some ways the absurdist playwrights are more conventional than Chekhov. With the exception of Beckett, they provide situations of tension that build up to climaxes—a rhythm of movement any audience can feel though perhaps it cannot understand. Beckett's works, like Chekhov's, are dramas of the loss of will, in which the unattainable salvation is deliberately vague, as in a dream, and in which language is man's sole occupation. Since salvation is transcendent and exterior to man, action is certainly needless; one sits and talks. In Chekhov the actions that occur are irrelevant to the willed desires of the characters. What is scrupulously denied is a catharsis of any recognizable sort, even a true dramatic climax. When climaxes are provided they are always out of focus, for Chekhov's people cannot see clearly enough to do what might be expected of them by ordinary standards. Treplev in *The Sea Gull* has already tried to kill himself, and so his successful suicide is somehow anticlimactic; moreover, the audience is denied, like Treplev, the meaning this action will have to the others. So the action is simply an action, and as long as it is not interpreted within the context of the play, it never achieves meaning. The climax of *The Three Sisters*—Tuzenbach's death in a duel—affirms the sisters' loss rather than tying it together in a single, compact image, the death being denied sentimental value and even meaning, for Irina does not love Tuzenbach. The climax of *The Cherry Orchard*—the merchant Lopakhin's revelation that it is he who has bought the estate on which his father was once a serf ("I bought it," he announces with pride and awe)—initiates wrong reactions from everyone, for Lopakhin is the central character and had wanted in some confused way recognition for what he had done; this leads into the strange fourth act, an act of abandonment and leavetaking conducted with the most banal of conversations. Technically, a climax occurs in each play, but thematically, it is somehow not the right climax. The true issues are always avoided. Only in *Uncle Vanya* does the "hero" accurately sight his enemy, but of course he is unable to kill him and unable to commit suicide. If there is a catharsis in any acceptable sense in Chekhov, it must be through the accumulation of detail and the revelation

120

of character, through the history of a given moment in terms of numbers of people and not simply, as in most drama, in terms of one or two people. The cathartic recognition of the relationship between the reality on stage and the reality it is meant to mirror in the real world makes the works art, but this art is difficult because it guides the emotional expectations of the audience up to a certain point and then baffles these expectations, allows a tragic situation to turn comic, denies its heroes or heroines the knowledge that would make them noble, and, strangest of all, deliberately scatters the audience's emotions among a group of people. If the audience could focus its sympathies upon one person, this person might achieve a kind of elevation; but in Chekhov it is rather the relationships between people and not the "realistics" of the people themselves that are of interest. Such art is difficult bcause no audience is prepared for it.

By contrast, such well-known absurdist plays as Ionesco's *The Bald Soprano, The Lesson,* and *The Chairs* are structured along lines that are almost anecdotal, in each case ending with a catharsis of violence in which the accumulated tensions are exorcized by complete irrationality. *The Killer,* Ionesco's most interesting long play, ends with a final scene that is really an act in itself, in which a fairly ordinary, intelligent, pseudoheroic man confronts the mysterious killer, a deformed, giggling creature, and is finally overcome by his "infinitely stubborn will." Despite the metaphysical poetry of Ionesco's images—his "arbitrary issues" that remind us of the private, privately created world of Kafka—the accumulation and release of tension in these plays is actually classic. The audience's emotions are guided by an expert hand. Ionesco is concerned with *change,* and despite

121

the difficulties one might have intellectually with this change, its emotional, visual reality is clear enough. He speaks of the two fundamental states of consciousness at the root of all his plays: feelings of evanescence and heaviness. Most often, "lightness changes to heaviness, transparence to thickness; the world weighs heavily; the universe crushes. . . . Matter fills everything, takes up all space, annihilates all liberty under its weight. . . . Speech crumbles." [2] If it is not matter precisely that annihilates, it is the savagery that weighs down upon the spiritual—the metamorphoses of men into beasts, never subtle, or the actual killing of characters onstage. In Chekhov this demonstration of the play's structure is never clear; the audience's emotions are dissipated, go off in several directions, cannot focus upon any single conflict. The meaning of Ionesco may be baffling, but the dramatic focus of his art is not. In Chekhov the meaning is perhaps inexplicable apart from the actual terms of the plays themselves, but the concentration of dramatic action is in itself baffling. Hence the notorious problems of staging Chekhov. When the dying old servant, Firs, limps in at the end of *The Cherry Orchard*, having been left alone in the big house by the departing characters, one does not know whether to laugh or cry; the conclusion is brilliantly appropriate, and yet impossible to define. Surely this is the real end of the "old order"—a faithful servant who sentimentally recalls serfdom, abandoned by his former owners without a second thought. But in another sense, a more theatrical sense, it is simply absurd, gratuitous and unexpected, and distracts attention from what has been supposed the main action: the effects of selling the estate upon the main characters.

In Ionesco the play ends abruptly because the charac-

ters, who are soulless, have been accepted simply as theatrical approximations of life in its ludicrous or mysterious sense, and the meaning of the work is ultimately abstract and universal; in Chekhov the play ends technically, but the characters, given life so scrupulously, carry
its meaning along with them and do not surrender it
when the curtain falls. The absurdist theater has limited
powers because its works are essentially parables whose
success or failure depends entirely upon the ingenuity of
the transformation of idea (for example, the idea that
man waits endlessly for his true life, his real self, his salvation) into arresting images, and, as parables, they can
evoke only an intellectual response in the audience. One
can laugh at Beckett's people, since they deliberately invite laughter, but one cannot share their sorrow because
it is not a human sorrow; it is a representation, at its most
sterile an allegorical representation, of real sorrow that
exists somewhere in the human world—a curious parallel
to the assumptions of the medieval morality play. In
Chekhov, even the most mysterious characters are made
real for us by some abrupt switching of point of view, so
that the character—Solyony or Charlotta—does not slip
safely into caricature. Chekhov's stage "looks" real
enough, and his characters speak a language that has the
surface formlessness of that of real life, but in essence his
conception of drama is more complex and more icono-
clastic than that of the absurdists, whose revolt is chiefly
in terms of a simplification of life and an attendant exaggeration of limited experiences.

One of the spectacular devices of the absurd stage is its
use of language. Ionesco was driven to write *The Bald
Soprano* out of his desire to express the "tragedy of lan-

123

guage"—the breakdown in communication that is a result of the failure of man to know himself, to relate himself meaningfully to other men and to his world. At bottom, one feels, this is another manifestation of the mourning for the old, dead gods, whose presence or assumed presence is necessary for man to remain man. Humanism is a failure, the absurdists say, because man is not "human," cannot know himself, therefore cannot control himself, and, above all, cannot control his world. In Beckett, the world cannot be controlled, and nothing happens; in Ionesco, the hallucinatory movement of the world cannot be controlled, for the hero who attempts to do so (Bérenger in *The Killer* and *Rhinoceros*) discovers in himself an unconscious collaboration with the forces of destruction. The stasis of ordinary humanity in the drama of the absurd is an extreme working-out of the dilemma of the humanist or liberal writer: how to create tragedy, which is predicated upon the uniqueness of human beings, in a leveled world in which all are equal and all are perhaps without value. The stupid anguish of Ionesco's characters is eloquence for our time; as Raymond Williams says in a study of liberal tragedy (the tragedy of the "heroic liberator opposed and destroyed by a false society"), when one identifies with the false society, the society cannot then be opposed or challenged by death, but must simply be confessed, forgiven, and lived with. Suffering is "separate and finally isolated"; the deadlock is absolute and we are all victims." [3]

The distortion and madness of language in the absurd theater relate, then, to the interior distortion and madness of a society that still can make itself understood on a conventional, cliché-ridden level. It is a theater of and for victims—creatures who have misplaced their souls or deliberately betrayed them—relating to an audience in the same condition that has not yet, as Nietzsche would say, heard the news. Their language reflects their deracination, for without absolute values the romantic imagination cannot endure sanity: it demands grotesque images, a frenzied dance of madness to express its anguish. If Chekhov does not seem romantic, it is because of his impersonality, his refusal to exaggerate or make particularly poetic the suffering his hollow people endure. Always their limitations are carefully exposed as self-induced limitations, not gross misfortunes that symbolize the evil of the universe. But the vision of man in absurdist drama and in Chekhov is similar, if not identical. The mournful poetry of *Waiting for Godot*—

"Have you not done tormenting me with your accused time? . . . One day, is that not enough for you, one day like any other day, he went dumb, one day I went blind, one day we'll go deaf, one day we were born, one day we'll die, the same day, the same second. . . . They give birth astride of a grave, the light gleams an instant, then it's night once more."

—is matched by the laments of a typical Chekhovian character (Andrei of *The Three Sisters* talking to a man who cannot hear well):

"Oh, where is it, where has it all gone, my past when I was young, gay, clever, when I dreamed and thought with grace, when my present and my future were lighted up with hope? Why is it that when we have barely begun to live, we grow dull, gray, uninteresting, lazy, indifferent, useless, unhappy. . . . Our town has been in existence now for two hundred years, there are a hundred thousand people in it, and not one who isn't exactly like all the others, not one saint . . . not one scholar, not one artist, no one in the least remarkable. . . . They just eat, drink, sleep, and then die . . . others are

125

born and they, too, eat, drink, sleep, and to keep from being stupefied by boredom, they relieve the monotony of life with their odious gossip, with vodka, cards . . . and an overwhelmingly vulgar influence weighs on the children, the divine spark is extinguished in them, and they become the same pitiful, identical corpses as their fathers and mothers."

Beckett's outcasts seem to arrive at once at their insights, making no progress toward any kind of enlightenment; Chekhov's people, involved as they are in a three-dimensional drama, move in a way that is less a progression than a devastation of illusion. Ionesco's people are victims of their incapacity for expression and are therefore less than human. At the end of *The Bald Soprano*, the Smiths and Martins yell furiously at each other, having achieved a kind of passionate rapport beneath the level of rationality, but the achievement of passion marks the end of their humanity. *The Chairs* is a play about nothing but words—the first part being concerned with half-expressed, private anecdotes, and the second part with the desperate, pathetic attempt to turn private experience into universal knowledge, mocked cruelly by Ionesco's mute Orator, who either betrays the Old Man or delivers his message precisely; in either case the "message" is lost. The traditional farewell of tragedy—Othello's final words, Antony's final words—is parodied here, for when life has lost its meaning and there is only "metaphysical emptiness," words have no value.

Chekhov's naturalism when it is most "natural" arouses in the audience the same sense of mystery that Ionesco's deliberate absurdity does. When Masha, who takes snuff and is hopelessly in love with the young writer Treplev, walks off stage in act 2 of *The Seagull* and has to drag her leg along because it has gone to sleep, the detail is both naturalistic and gratuitously absurd; so also is the snoring of Sorin in the same scene. The governess Charlotta of *The Cherry Orchard*, who eats cucumbers that she carries in her pocket and performs bizarre sleight-of-hand tricks, remains inexplicable. In *The Three Sisters*, the fugue-like pronouncement of major themes, desultory as it is, is yet interrupted by the solemn recitation of "facts": "And in Moscow . . . some merchants were eating pancakes; one of them, who ate forty, it seems died. It was either forty or fifty, I don't remember," "Balzac was married in Berdichev," and "Tsisikar. Smallpox is raging there." The gloomy fourth act is punctuated by Chebutykin's singing of "Ta-ra-ra boom-de-ay." The large groupings of people on Chekhov's stage make possible mock choral comments that pass judgments upon the main characters unintentionally. But essentially Chekhov's characters pass judgment on themselves. The first act of *The Three Sisters* begins with a birthday celebration, yet its tone is oddly elegaic. Olga, the oldest sister, says at once: "Father died a year ago today." The entire play, spreading out as it does over a period of years, is a working out of the significance of that fact. "Father," the dead general, the intellectual who "oppressed" education on his children to prepare them for a sort of life absolutely unavailable, is equated with Moscow, the paradise, the lost Eden, the lost "home," and the sisters' willed obsession with this ghostly lost home will cause them to lose their real home. But the several statements of rapturous yearning for Moscow at the very start of the play are undercut by the seemingly incidental remarks of the men who are visiting: "Like hell he did!" "Of course, that's nonsense," "With one hand I can lift only fifty pounds, but with two I can lift a hundred and eighty or

even two hundred pounds . . . ," and "For falling hair
. . . two ounces of naphthaline to half a bottle of
spirits . . . dissolve and apply daily. . . ." Mixed in
with these phrases are the line of poetry that keeps running through Masha's mind and that will become an expression of her love—"A green oak by a curved seashore
. . . upon that oak a golden chain . . ."—and the
lines from a fable that Solyony quotes, anticipating both
his and Protopopov's destruction of the dream of this
first act—"He no sooner cried 'alack' than the bear was
on his back. . . ."

In Ionesco's *The Bald Soprano*, all conversation is
nonsense. It does not point toward any thematic sense,
but is content to be a hilarious expression of the nonsense people do speak:

MR. SMITH
One walks on his feet, but one heats with electricity or coal.
MR. MARTIN
He who sells an ox today, will have an egg tomorrow.
MRS. SMITH
In real life, one must look out the window.
MRS. MARTIN
One can sit down on a chair, when the chair doesn't have
any.
MR. SMITH
One must always think of everything.
MR. MARTIN
The ceiling is above, the floor is below.

These aphorisms, which make as much sense as most
clichés, then degenerate into pure sound, noise, bestial-
ity, as the Smiths and the Martins yell furiously at each
other. One regrets the unnecessary conclusion of "It's
not that way, it's over here"—the "it" obviously meaning

sanity—but the decision to end the play with the Martins taking the Smiths' places is an excellent one, emphasizing as it does the endlessness of this purgatorial condition. For Ionesco and Chekhov the condition of man is rather like Beckett's notion of the spherical purgatory, in which one can never make any progress and the "shadow in the end is no better than the substance." [4] That the "reality" is no better than its appearance would suggest, and that the appearance, which seems preferable to the reality precisely because of its being illusory, is ultimately "no better," is an ironic inversion of what one might expect; man is willfully deceived by his language and his conception of the world, but this deception does him no good because he himself lacks the imagination to give it beauty.

As in Ionesco and Beckett, one finds in Chekhov the substitution of language for action. All his plays are demonstrations of the impotence of will. The doctor in *Uncle Vanya* works very hard, hasn't had a single day free in ten years, but he regards his present work as meaningless drudgery and looks to the misty future for a righting of present horrors. For most of the others, talk is unrelated to action. When Irina speaks ecstatically of "work," she is unable to anticipate her very natural and inevitable disgust with the work she can actually find to do. Vershinin, entrapped in an ugly marriage, echoes Astrov's prophecy that salvation lies somewhere in the future: "In two or three hundred years life on this earth will be unimaginably beautiful, wonderful. Man needs such a life, and so long as it is not here, he must foresee it, expect it, dream about it, prepare for it." The sisters and their brother, Andrei, learned French, German, and English from their father—the means of expressing themselves in three languages besides their own—and yet of course they have nothing to express; Masha says: "In this town, to know three languages is a needless luxury—not even a luxury, but a sort of superfluous appendage, like a sixth finger." In *The Cherry Orchard*, language is hardly shared by the characters. The merchant Lopakhin explains what the family must do in order to save their estate, but they cannot understand him. As the catastrophe nears, they expend themselves in useless dialogue calculated to distract them from reality. Even the student Trofimov, who expresses once again Chekhov's own hopes for an ideal future, is an "eternal student" who knows nothing of life and whose high-sounding words are perhaps ludicrous. He says of his relationship with Anya:

"We are above love. To avoid the petty and the illusory, which prevent our being free and happy—that is the aim and meaning of life. Forward! We are moving irresistibly toward the bright star that burns in the distance! Forward! Do not fall behind, friends!"

Anya, delighted, exclaims: "How well you talk!" And the emphasis surely is on the word "talk," an ironic emphasis since it implies the young man's own illusory condition. The same sort of substitution of talk for action is found everywhere in the absurdist theater, most notably in Beckett's plays (and in his novels as well). In Ionesco's short play, *The Lesson*, a curious transformation of the eclipsing of life by language is effected when the tyrannical professor kills his student with the word "knife" —having complete control of the meanings of words, he controls the girl's reactions to them and hence her life. The totalitarian misuse of language suggested by the professor's omnipotence is sounded also in *The Killer*, where a fascistic woman named Mother Peep demonstrates the facility of believing that stupidity is intelligence, cowardice is bravery, clear-sightedness is blindness, liquidation is "only physical."

The Three Sisters demonstrates most clearly the progress of disintegration that is the basis of most absurdist plays. After the substitution of language for action there is the substitution of false rhetoric for the truth. When Olga says happily at the beginning of the play that she longs passionately to go "home" again (to Moscow) and that this dream "keeps growing stronger and stronger," one accepts this as perfectly truthful and admirable. When the same refrain is repeated throughout the play, however, it takes on a sinister and ironic note the sisters themselves do not understand. Thus, at the conclusion of act 2, while Natasha runs out to a very real man, Irina is left alone to yearn for her illusory paradise. "To Moscow!" she cries, and the cry is by now discomforting. The end of act 3 has Irina, the youngest, again yearning for Moscow, but by now she has had to agree to a marriage she does not really want: "I'll marry him, I'm willing, only let us go to Moscow! I implore you, let us go! There's nothing in the world better than Moscow!" Now the longing is hysterical and is intended to cover up the knowledge she has expressed earlier—that everything has somehow gone wrong, that she has forgotten her Italian, that they will never, never see Moscow. The end of the play has the sisters grouped together and consoling themselves with rhetoric, much like Sonya at the end of *Uncle Vanya*. We have here a brutal counterpointing of idealism and nihilism, as the sisters hear the military music and say that they want to live, that "it seems as if just a little more and we shall know why we live, why we suffer . . . ," and the old doctor sits by "amiably," undisturbed by the death of Tuzenbach and singing "Ta-ra-ra boom-de-ay, sit on the curb I may"; the last impression of this extraordinary play is one of frozen dialectic, intelligence deceiving itself with words and balanced by a mindlessness that uses words quite aptly to express its curb-sitting or moral paralysis, an image for the sisters as well as the doctor. Indeed, it is their idealism, their failure to make concrete and therefore active the words they use so charmingly, that has ruined their "real" lives. Natasha, who cannot talk well at all and whose French is embarrassingly poor, is significantly victorious over the sisters. Other symptoms of disintegration reflected in language are the change from the love duets of the second act (Masha and Vershinin; Irina and Tuzenbach) to the monologues of the last acts (the doctor's soliloquy on his ruined life; Andrei's in the presence of a deaf man); the interruptions, aimless talk, and the jokes of Solyony's that always miss their mark; the *non sequiturs* that are at once amusing and unsettling, suggesting as they do a serious failure of sane communication. Chekhov's plays are tragedies of language, like Ionesco's, assaults against the conventional language, which disguises by its very conventionality the hollowness of those who use it.

Most interesting of all the similarities between the Chekhovian and the *avant-garde* theater is the use of the "arbitrary issue" as poetic image. In absurdist theater the arbitrary issue is that which, despite its apparent inadequacy, is to carry the burden of the character's obsession. In Adamov's *Le Ping-Pong*, it is a pinball machine that captivates the imaginations of two men who grow old playing it, wasting their lives, transforming their natural human impulses toward transcendence into nonsensical trivialities about the machine itself. As Esslin notes in his excellent study of the play, the work is a powerful image of the "alienation of man through the worship of a false objective" [5]—the machine itself an obvious metaphor for anything that captivates men's lives without being worth the sacrifice. In Ionesco as well the arbitrary issue is that which is "given" without explanation: one must find out whether Mallot spelled his name with a "t" or a "d," one must get the growing corpse out of the apartment, one must resist to the end the metamorphosis into a rhinoceros. The images are not significant in themselves (except as theater), but only in what they suggest. This conception of writing differs from, for instance, the very real and not at all arbitrary issues of Ibsen, attacking the hypocrisy of society in *Ghosts*, or of Strindberg, passionately attacking the vampirish female. As if the world no longer offered real issues, these several playwrights create grotesque and parodying issues that will dominate their characters' imaginations and, when the play is successful, the audience's imagination as well. Such theater is really poetry, as Kafka's works are poetry: the creation of a sustained image that is the vehicle for symbolic meaning, yet never glibly contained by this meaning. But because the image is necessarily private and not social, historical, or mythical, the meaning must be expanded by the audience, which as a kind of unified consciousness can no longer be content to know—as Picasso says of most people—only what they already know. The difficulty with absurdist theater is its deliberate refusal to tell us what we already know, its unheroic heroes and unvillainous villains, its mock plots, its insistence upon baffling expectation, its taking over the prat-falls and rapid dialogue of vaudeville entertainment while leaving behind the "honest" foolishness. But as poetry, its images are closer to Pound's definition of the image than are, perhaps, such readily acceptable images as the paper lantern in Williams' *A Streetcar Named Desire* and the doomed bird in *Miss Julie*. In 1913 Pound defined the "image" as "that which presents an intellectual and emotional complex in an instant of time. . . . It is the presentation of such a 'complex' instantaneously which gives that sense of sudden liberation; that sense of freedom from time limits and space limits; that sense of sudden growth, which we experience in the presence of the greatest works of art." [6] The Imagists themselves created no images that broke so completely from the conventionally "poetic" as did the dramatists of the absurd.

In traditional theater the central issue is always acted upon; this is the only means of plot. One finally kills the king, though at great expense; one manages to marry the inevitable person; one breaks free from husband, children, and hypocritical society. Generally, in Chekhov and the absurd dramatists, the central issue is either not understood or not acted upon or both. The cherry orchard has all the makings of a symbol except—unlike the stuffed seagull in the earlier play—its symbolism points in several directions. It is various things to various people, and yet in itself it does not exist; it has no meaning. Never does anyone see the cherry orchard for what it is; they see wasted opportunities for making money, or they see ghostly faces in it, whether the student Trofimov's vision of the faces of serfs or Madame Ranevskaya's vision of her dead mother walking in it. They are capable of seeing only what they bring to it, of seeing only themselves. And when the orchard is finally sold, when the catastrophe happens, there is a queerly inappropriate relief; Gayev, though totally displaced by the change, says cheerfully:

"Yes, indeed, everything is all right now. Before the cherry orchard was sold we were all worried and miserable, but afterward, when the question was finally settled once and for all, everybody calmed down and felt quite cheerful."

One is reminded of Mann's famous definition of irony in his essay, "Goethe and Tolstoy": a technique that glances at both sides, playing "slyly and irresponsibly among opposites." With such irony there is no possibility of sentimental excess, since the writer does not choose sides.

If this is so, the theatergoer wants to ask, then what is the play about? Why has it been written? That the apparent central issue of a work should be declared quite trivial and insignificant after all the words and tears exerted for it is an extraordinary event in literature. It is as if the conventional form of art were calling itself into question, calling its very reason for existence into question, or calling, at least, the conventional audience's expectations into question. If it is ever appropriate to talk of genres in close relationship to actual works of art, one might say that for the tragic vision, deadly seriousness must always surround this central issue, and what the play undertakes is of real concern not only within the context of the play, but symbolically for its audience. Tragedy is a sacred art form. When self-consciousness or doubt or an impulse toward self-parody enter, tragedy disintegrates. In Chekhov this is precisely the case.

As in Beckett, the less tangible the means of salvation, the greater the urgency for salvation becomes. The intelligent human beings of such drama, caught in the purgatorial present, can only *talk*; it is the stupid—Natasha, Solyony, Arkadina, the professor of *Uncle Vanya*—who live on some level of existence, forcing others to submit to their wills, the simple fact of their being able to live involving a death for others. As one element gains strength, so another element loses strength. The ghostliness of the central issue or image in Chekhov gives way abruptly to the flagrant mystery of the central issue of a play like *Godot*. Godot as image approaches the unfathomable just as Melville's white whale does—the former by its very absence, the latter by its tremendously detailed presence. Chekhov's imagery is more conventional than that of the absurdists, of course, since he is committed to a naturalistic stage, but his use of the image is similar: the truly poetic image whose meaning, as Pound says, gives one a sense of liberation and sudden growth by refusing to confine itself—in other words, to the easily explicable.

If there is intellectual debate in the theater of the absurd it is, like the "intellectual" discussions in Chekhov, ironic, exaggerated, and foolish, coming as it does at the point in history at which philosophy is divorced from the transcendental values it once tried to discover or support. Hence debate, talk, and duets of dialogue become meaningless, and characters are their own chorus, speaking and commenting endlessly upon their own speech. Are there images behind this speech? Are there realities behind these images? The prevailing tone in existential literature

136

is that of mystery. In this art a strange, dissipated action, or the memory or vague desire for action, has replaced the older, more vital, ritualistic concerns of the stage. Chekhov and the absurdists remain true to their subject —life—by refusing to reduce their art to a single emotion and idea.

6

YEATS:
Violence, Tragedy,
Mutability

[Divinity] moves outside our antinomies, it may be our lot to
worship in terror.

Yeats, *"Prometheus Unbound"*

Like Nietzsche, Yeats resists systematic definitions even when he attempts a conscious unity of thought; one senses in his work an unconscious repugnance to the formality of a completed gesture, an unambiguous vision. Even his most celebrated concept, the mysterious "Unity of Being," cannot be defined except as rhetorical tautology, the kind of abstraction Yeats despised. For he defines in 1937 his faith in his own Christ, "that Unity of Being Dante compared to a perfectly proportioned human body," yet goes on to say that this conception is an imminent one, differing from man to man and age to age.[1] Beneath A Vision and its celebrated complexities is the phenomenal power of this mystical unity, which seems to have involved for Yeats extreme hatred as well as extreme love. Yet it is inexplicable to the speculating Yeats himself: the "harsh geometry" of A Vision remains an incomplete interpretation.

Prophetic and apocalyptic, Yeats is yet intensely personal, his obsessions refining themselves until the cult of personality becomes a kind of mythologizing release. The romantic impulse toward the apotheosis of the ordinary, the immediate, the existential, is at constant odds with the classical, intellectual, harshly mathematical impulse in Yeats to turn everything to stone, to the clarity of gold and marble. And surely one of his most famous images—the golden bird—remains a paradox. "Once out of nature I shall never take/ My bodily form from any natural thing"—yet the form so carefully chosen is certainly, as Sturge Moore pointed out, the form of a natural thing in spite of the hammered gold and gold enameling. Yeats cannot project his being into so starkly abstract an image as those he thought comparable to his system in A Vision, the "stylistic arrangements of experience" similar to the cubes of Wyndham Lewis and the ovoids in the sculpture of Brancusi. The human imagination, in becoming abstract, seeks its metamorphosis on the animal level.[2]

In addition to the rich paradoxes of the poems and plays, the critic must contend with yet another voice—the patient, rational, and supposedly helpful voice of the essays. But the respectful intellect of the essays, with its elaborate accounting of the passage of the soul in Indian mysticism and asceticism, and its patient consideration of the philosophy of Berkeley and of others, is brutally undercut by the poems of the same years—the "Crazy Jane" sequence, for instance.

In his last poems Yeats moves toward a contemplative and dispassionate assertion of the joy that can arise out of tragedy, and the poem that ends his career, "Under Ben Bulben," leaves us with the image of a cold eye looking upon life and death equally, unmoved, like the golden bird of "Sailing to Byzantium" that sings equally of what is past, or passing, or to come. Yet the jagged tonalities of the last poems will not be reconciled by the theoretical claim for a dispassionate unity, just as certain poems, examined individually, will not support their apparent themes. Yeats's genius lies not in his ability to hammer his multiple thoughts into unity, but rather in his faithful accounting of the impossibility—which may lead one to the edge of madness—of bringing together aesthetic theory and emotional experience. His final work is characterized by irony, but more importantly by an incomplete blend of the "tragic" and the "mutable." What is tragic is intended to transcend or in some way justify the suffering Yeats or his legendary personae have experienced, and takes its most frequent immortality in the shape of a work of art; what is mutable is all that is left out, all that will not fit in—in short, life itself, the material of art itself.

That bewildering play, *The Herne's Egg* (1938), operates rather mechanically upon what must have been imagined as a strictly symbolic pattern, offering us a priestess, a divine being in the shape of a bird, seven ravishers of the priestess, and a bizarre and violent ending. Yet the last lines—"All that trouble and nothing to show for it,/ Nothing but just another donkey"—undercut the ritualistic pretensions of the work, and may be intended as a commentary on Yeats's deepest conception of his material: all this trouble for just another donkey, just another existing creature, without meaning.[3] Similar ironic switches of tone or point of view are found in many of the poems, particularly the amazing final poems, and an investigation of the tension between philosophic commitment and artistic production will bear out the essential ambiguity of Yeats's imagination. Is it possible to achieve an organic penetration of the human faculty of reason with the human faculty of the imagination, an essential relationship between the "objects of perception" and the mode of perception itself?

In *"Prometheus Unbound"* (1932), Yeats states surprisingly that it is not Blake, after all, who most shaped his life, but Shelley: a visionary, a "psychic" being, but an unconverted man.[4] And he speaks of Balzac changing men's lives, saving Yeats himself from the obsessive pursuit of absolute and external beauty that, to strike a balance, would have required "hatred as absolute." His art has been carefully imagined, carefully worked and reworked; legendary, archetypal beings have been given new life in order to transform the secular age into something approaching holiness, or at any rate into an age that can, through the study of Yeats's monumental verse, appreciate the passing of holiness.

Yet the effort seems out of proportion to the primary, fundamental argument of the poems. For the poems are continually dehumanizing their subjects, even to the point of thwarting the demands of a gay tragedy; in "The Gyres" Yeats insists upon the joyousness of tragedy, he insists that those witnesses to the modern chaos look on and laugh "in tragic joy," without sighs or tears:

> For painted forms or boxes of make-up
> In ancient tombs I sighed, but not again;
> What matter? Out of cavern comes a voice,
> And all it knows is that one word 'Rejoice!'

The refrain "What matter?" is set against the vision of a world in which "irrational streams of blood are staining earth," where "Empedocles has thrown all things about." The soul of man has coarsened, approaching the darkness of nothing; yet the gyres will bring round all things once again, disinterring the dead. In "Lapis Lazuli," which Yeats believed to be one of his most successful poems, the theme of Nietzschean gaiety is continued. We must believe that our sufferings are enacted upon a tragic stage, and that our human gaiety transfigures "all that dread." The poem ends, like the "Ode on a Grecian Urn," with a contemplation of a work of art, the Chinamen carved in lapis lazuli, whom Yeats imagines as staring down upon the tragic scene of temporal life with "ancient, glittering eyes" that are gay.

The basic difficulty with this position is its abstracting of the human, its forcing upon animate life a certain theoretical and ultimately epistemological shape. For no matter what aesthetic position we finally give to Yeats, the very fact of his various responses to formal unity and "profane perfection" will contradict it. Thus these poems, insisting upon an impersonal logic that transcends human suffering, can be read in the context of certain other poems and plays as ironic statements, partial statements, to be qualified or questioned by the poet.

145

So long as the world is conceived dynamically one cannot come to rest, either in a piece of lapis lazuli or in a formal, completed tragedy. Like Wallace Stevens, who inherited many of Yeats's preoccupations with the duality of man's imaginative response to the world, Yeats knows that:

> We keep coming back and coming back
> To the real: to the hotel instead of the hymns
> That fall upon it out of the wind . . .[5]

Approaching death inspires the poet to a frenzy of self-fabrication. He will "make his soul," compelling it to take on the colossal tragic shapes of Lear and Cuchulain, and the "second-best" shape of the wild old wicked man. In the form of a pilgrim he journeys to the purgatorial world of the dead, only to be told in reply to his questions, *Fol de rol de rolly O*. The knowledge available to man, and that becomes in turn the knowledge the poet will give back to the world, is nonsense, verbal nonsense—*Fol de rol de rolly O*. The formal perfection of tragedy is now lost. Ironically, the poet understands in "The Municipal Gallery Revisited," in the very place of formal images and "deep-rooted things," that the mathematical movement of the gyres does not promise any human salvation, any human meaning at all. It is the earth itself that is lost:

> And I am in despair that time may bring
> Approved patterns of women or of men
> But not that selfsame excellence again.

Two difficult poems, "The Statues" and "News for the Delphic Oracle," offer us twin and warring interpretations of life. What is reality? Yeats's central question, his maddening question, deals with the extension and limitation of reality, man's power and man's will (for, as he states arrogantly in "The Tower," "Death and life were not/ Till man made up the whole,/ Made lock, stock and barrel/ Out of his bitter soul . . .") in confrontation with the silence of nothingness, the ultimate chaos that has no meaning and is not concerned with meaning. Not human evil, but inhuman chaos, is for Yeats, as it was for Shakespeare, the supreme horror. Therefore, what lies beyond the human imagination, being horrible, must be constantly given a shape, "named."

In "The Statues" we are told of artists, men who "with a mallet or a chisel" modeled the speculative philosophers' calculations and "put down/ All Asiatic vague immensities." It is not knowledge that redeems, for "knowledge increases unreality"; it is, rather, the power of the creative imagination, whether working in stone or with words or with certain noble men of Ireland that is important. The switch to "we Irish" is surprising, even in a poem by Yeats, since the poem has dealt with so vast a landscape and signals the poet's ironically arrogant conclusion to the metaphysical problem he has brought up. Born into an ancient race but "thrown upon this filthy modern tide," it is yet possible for the Irish to climb to their proper level in order to "trace/ The lineaments of a plummet-measured face." That is, the Irish can read with their fingers the shape of a heroic face or personality and trace in the darkness an archetypal vision that will redeem them, since passion is equal to creation; "passion could bring character enough," and brings the living to press their lips against a work of art, as if it were indeed living. Here the living, the Irish, are to remake themselves in the image of a colossal vision. It is form-

147

lessness that is to be conquered, a climbing out of the spawning fury of the modern world.[6]

"News for the Delphic Oracle," however, imagines a pastoral dimension where all the "golden codgers" lay, old men refined of the mire and fury of human blood, where the dew itself is silver. In this paradise of completed forms, of stilled gestures, everyone sighs. Plotinus, having swum the buffeting seas of "The Delphic Oracle upon Plotinus" (*Words for Music Perhaps*), now stretches and yawns. These "Innocents" relive their ancient patterns, "dreaming back through their lives," until the burden of their humanity is finally thrown off. Like the spirits of "Byzantium," they have achieved "death-in-life," "life-in-death." But the third stanza focuses upon the union of Peleus and Thetis, the union of bodies and of beautiful parts of bodies. Thetis' "limbs are delicate as an eyelid" and Peleus' eyes are blinded with tears. The "intolerable" music of Pan falls upon them and suddenly the poem breaks into a confusion of jarring images, of finite, joyous, profane parts that contradict the world of golden forms:

> Foul goat-head, brutal arm appear,
> Belly, shoulder, bum,
> Flash fishlike; nymphs and satyrs
> Copulate in the foam.

The poem ends with this violent activity, an activity that hardly seems willed by human beings so much as by parts of bodies, the frenzy of the flesh one with the foaming sea. It is a stunning reversal of the poem's opening, where the "golden" people lay sighing in their completion. Their choir of love with its "sacred laurel crowns"

148

and its Pythagorean beauty contrasts feebly with the music of Pan, felt as intolerable.

That the static resolution of human complexity cannot be sustained is examined in the famous Byzantium poems, the "Byzantium" of *The Winding Stair* taken as a qualification of the "Sailing to Byzantium" of *The Tower*. For here purgation effects its magic only at night, when the images of the day recede, and though the miracle of a golden bird can crow like the cocks of Hades (imagined as real birds?), it is curiously enough "embittered" by the moon—though why the miraculous bird should be embittered by the changing, subjective moon, since it is immune to mortality, is puzzling. And the poem itself ends with images that yet "fresh images beget," the rage and wilderness of the foaming sea, which no amount of human artifice can transform into art. So the poem works itself out, like "News for the Delphic Oracle," as a deeply ironic turning upon itself, a drama of the challenge of two opposing dimensions whose tragic irony is visible only to the poet himself. The dialectic is grasped only by the poet: the world of artifice is immune to change and does not exist; the world of nature is immune to abstraction and exists only in dying generations, without control or consciousness.

Therefore Yeats achieves, even through his intensely autobiographical and confessional poems, a rendering of the self's basic impersonality, at the point at which it enters art. Here he finds, to his distress, the very negation of the younger Yeats. For at the core of his mature art is the puzzled insistence upon the formlessness of all substance and the insubstantial nature of all form—in short, a vision of human tragedy destroyed by mutability.

149

It is no wonder that events in Yeats's work are violent, his images far-fetched and grotesque. Very little has been said about the madness of some of his images. His superhuman Cuchulain will die at the hands of a beggar, for twelve pennies, and will find himself transformed into something wildly antithetical to his soul:

> There floats out there
> The shape that I shall take when I am dead,
> My soul's first shape, a soft feathery shape,
> And is not that a strange shape for the soul
> Of a great fighting-man? [7]

Cuchulain is answered only by the senile muttering of the Blind Man, who is trying to behead him. When Cuchulain dies he dies into song, the singing of a bird; his symbolic death "dies" us into the modern age, its music being that of some Irish fair. A Street-Singer tells of what the harlot sang to the beggar-man, recalling "what centuries have passed" since these heroic men lived. Cuchulain himself wakes in the poem of 1939, "Cuchulain Comforted," where the "violent and famous" man must sew his shroud in the company of convicted cowards who have died in fear. He becomes one of them, he who in life had been their opposite; he sings with them, changing his throat into the throat of a bird, for only in such profound humiliation can his life grow sweeter. It is a conclusion like that of *The Herne's Egg*—ironic and ambiguous. "I think profound philosophy must come from terror," Yeats says in the essay-broadcast, "Modern Poetry," of 1936. Whatever geometrical structure he has imagined for man and history, whatever fate appears to control individuals, it is ultimately the abyss that silences all questions:

An abyss opens under our feet; inherited convictions, the presuppositions of our thoughts . . . drop into the abyss. Whether we will or no we must ask the ancient questions: Is there reality anywhere? Is there a God? Is there a Soul? We cry with the Indian Sacred Book: "They have put a golden stopper into the neck of the bottle; pull it! Let out reality!" [8]

"The Man and the Echo" is another of Yeats's poems about death. Intensely personal, almost desperate, it shouts its secret in a place of stone:

> All that I have said and done,
> Now that I am old and ill,
> Turns into a question till
> I lie awake night after night
> And never get the answers right.

He questions his personal role in history, his effect upon certain people's lives. To what extent was he responsible for Irishmen shot by the English? (Auden's famous line, "poetry makes nothing happen"—in "In Memory of W. B. Yeats"—is a curiously simplistic resolution of Yeats's specific doubts. One of the crucial points about Yeats's life and work is that poetry *does* make something happen.) All seems to him evil; simply to die would be to shirk "the spiritual intellect's great work." What is desired is a single, clear view that arranges an entire life. He wants to stand in judgment on his own soul, yet he ends by asking, "What do we know but that we face/ One another in this place?" and even this beautiful, helpless thought is destroyed by the sudden plundering of nature:

> Up there some hawk or owl has struck,
> Dropping out of sky or rock,

151

> A stricken rabbit is crying out,
> And its cry distracts my thought.

Understanding himself a great poet, having conceived of himself in a great tradition, Yeats is nevertheless distracted by so commonplace and brutal an event. It is reality itself, the impersonal and gratuitous, the ever-changing, the unheroic, that cheats him of a final form. A violent gesture is the final gesture, simply because it silences all that has come before. Violence will disarm the tragic player, whether it rises out of his own body or out of the body of nature. It reminds us of the quiet, gentle ending of the ambitious and proud "Tower," when Yeats's death will seem no more than the clouds of the sky at twilight or "a bird's sleepy cry/ Among the deepening shades."

The most the poet can hope for is a kind of equanimity with the powerful chaos of nature. In "High Talk" and "The Circus Animals' Desertion," Yeats dismisses his creations as "all metaphor," "those stilted boys, that burnished chariot,/ Lion and woman and the Lord knows what":

> Malachi Stilt-Jack am I, whatever I learned has run wild,
> From collar to collar, from stilt to stilt, from father to child.
> All metaphor, Malachi, stilts and all. A barnacle goose
> Far up in the stretches of night; night splits and the dawn breaks loose;
> I, through the terrible novelty of light, stalk on, stalk on;
> Those great sea-horses bare their teeth and laugh at the dawn.

("High Talk")

Here the poet's ego manages a difficult balance with the prodigious and unthinking forms of nature. The barnacle goose has the magical power to break loose the dawn, which will take place regardless of the poet's words; the poet's triumph is to "stalk on" through the "terrible novelty of light," keeping his own place, his own proper dark, while the sea-horses—perfect images of energy, like the nymphs and satyrs in the foam—laugh at the breaking of a new day. The poet's activity, his stalking, is a kind of animal activity; he must imitate the animals in order to partake of their power.[9]

One of Yeats's most beautiful poems is "The Circus Animals' Desertion." Here he confesses that his own "animals" are no more than emblematic; they have not the power of real animals, real energy. Their existence has come from the poet's own bitterness, his starvation for life, the dreams that resulted from his own deprivation. "Heart-mysteries" give rise to dreams that, in turn, enchant the poet, until he dreams several moves from reality—he himself betraying the mighty Cuchulain, for it is ultimately the symbolic Cuchulain that engrosses Yeats, his own creation: "Players and painted stage took all my love,/ And not those things that they were emblems of." The poet is able to make such images masterful and complete, simply because they are images and not reality. He creates them out of the "purity" of his mind, having refined them out of their grosser origins. Thus, the sublimative poetic process is seen to be a betrayal of nature, or an inability to deal with nature itself. Yeats's statement of 1900, in "The Symbolism of Poetry," that "Solitary men make and unmake mankind, and even the world itself, for does not 'the eye altering alter all'?" seems the remark of a very young and ambitious artist; it is the central doctrine of Yeats's poetry, yet it cannot bear a confrontation with the dynamic world.

When the world and the self collide, the marketable drama is epistemological but, more than that, it is a moral confrontation—jarring and devastating to the ego.[10] In his essay *"Prometheus Unbound,"* Yeats speaks of the incomplete art of Shelley, where "sex is sublimated to an unearthly receptivity"; the poet is compelled to imagine whatever "seemed dark, destructive, indefinite."[11] Shelley is like Beardsley, who explains a compulsion to include something obscene in his drawings: "Something compels me to sacrifice to Priapus." The artist, acting upon his own sense of autonomy, is nevertheless forced to "secret the obscene" in some corner of his art; sublimation is a possibility only when the artist denies his basic self. Sublimation is a "ladder" but when the ladder is gone, the poet must acknowledge the origin of all his art, "in the foul rag-and-bone shop of the heart."

Infidelity to the earth is the most destructive of sins in the imagination of Nietzsche, whom Yeats was reading with great excitement as early as 1902.[12] Zarathustra resembles one of Yeats's rambling old poets, a prophetic and skeptical "wild old man" who teaches the holiness of the human will, a "new pride"; the ego, the "creating, willing, valuing ego, which is the measure and value of things."[13] Nietzsche attempts to bring together the chaotic objects of man's perception and man's perception itself through the concept of the "will," a "will to power" in its most masculine, selfless, and generous sense— a joining of man's energy with the energy of the universe, a refusal to create illusory worlds of God and morality where there is nothing. Nietzsche rebels against the great tradition of Western philosophy that asserts the primacy of thought and logic, the possibility of systematic knowledge, the fundamental workings of causal relationships themselves, the basis of science, of a certain kind of art, of morality—to him the permanent, Being itself, is only a parable, an "empty fiction." [14] In a parable of his own, Zarathustra talks of the river that, in ordinary times, seems peaceful and contained by its banks and bridges; no one believes in the prophet's warning, "Everything is in flux." In the winter the river is frozen and the prophet is further denounced by all of the world, which claims, "Does not everything *stand still?*" But nature cannot stand still. The spring thaw will come and the river will overflow and destroy its bridges and railings. Everything is in continual flux; civilization itself is eroded constantly by the will of man.[15] It is possible for Nietzsche to entertain contradictory thoughts at the same time because he views the intellect as superficial, the creator of values and truth and also their destroyer, the measure of all human things. Yeats lacks Nietzsche's originality and his philosophical brilliance, but his attempt to deal with certain Nietzschean doctrines in poetic form shows how very powerfully such ideas can be transformed into art. Nietzsche himself remains an indifferent poet—he is too unashamed of his emotions.

Essentially, the thematic structure of a typical poem or play gives us a timeless setting, a sense of ritualistic order, which is broken in upon by violence in some form—the violence of men or of nature. *Calvary, Purgatory,* the Cuchulain cycle, even *Deirdre,* among others, bear this out. The various claims of the artist, the supposed controller of will, are thwarted by the materials of his art that continue in their natural currents and cannot be measured by him. In "The Curse of Cromwell" Yeats laments the passing of "the lovers and the dancers" beaten into clay, the accelerating meanness of the modern world. But a certain realization destroys his heart, "because it proves that things both can and cannot be"— that the objects of his desire still exist, still hold him in thrall though they are dead and he living. But the communion with the dead is only an illusion; the poet must wake, finding himself alone much like the grieving old woman in "Her Vision in the Wood":

> But I woke in an old ruin that the winds howled through;
> And when I pay attention I must out and walk
> Among the dogs and horses that understand my talk.
> > *O what of that, O what of that,*
> > *What is there left to say?*

The way of solitude may be the way of madness. Both Nietzsche and Yeats utilize masks that are, at times, mad; having no language on a human level, they are driven to commune with the beasts. Their worlds are ones in which violent clashes, reversals, and rejections are common, though unpredicted; what is significant is that the poet is always alone. Suffering does not draw us into a brotherhood of men. Though tragedy seems to break down the "dykes that separate man from man," [16] the experience is aesthetic rather than humanistic. It is the strange "emptiness" of tragedy that appeals to us, not its communal nature; neither Nietzsche nor Yeats makes anything of the ideal of shared suffering, common to the religions of the world.[17]

"Under Ben Bulben" returns to a consideration of the power of art, where "completeness of . . . passions" may win immortality, where man passes through a series of reincarnations, and where poets and sculptors must do the work of giving form to mankind. Yet even in this more conventional poem, ending with a prophetic hope for Irish poets, there is the qualification of stanza 3, which assigns an ultimate value to the time when "all words are said" and man's will erupts in violence. Paradoxically, the loss of language results in man's "partial mind" becoming completed and his heart becoming peaceful, for

> Even the wisest man grows tense
> With some sort of violence
> Before he can accomplish fate,
> Know his work or choose his mate.

Yeats's works are filled with violence. It is the flooding of the ego by the fury of the veins, a sudden and irrevocable alliance with nature's chaos. The most general associations we have with Yeats's poetry are two—the golden bird on the Byzantine bough and the rape of Leda. It is significant that these two opposing images come to mind most readily, for they represent the obsessive claims of Yeats's art.[18] Had he truly believed his early assertions in the 1901 essay, "Magic"—that our minds belong to a single mind, that our memories belong to the memory of nature itself, and that this great mind and great memory can be evoked by symbols—he would have remained a minor poet, content with the vague evocation of a mysterious and ineffable unity. Instead, his deepest instinct is to reject unity while he yearns for it; not only does he seem to reject it philosophically, like Nietzsche, but he seems to reject it emotionally as well. The epic and the dramatic impulses in Yeats far outweigh the lyric impulse, and that is why all his writings inform one another; the *Collected Works* constitute Yeats's being itself, the justification for his existence. But within the

157

projected framework of a single book no single unity is possible, apart from the unity necessarily imposed upon the work by the passage of time, which the poet is anxious to record. The intellectual concept of unity is impossible for the artist to achieve, except at great cost to his art. It is not paradoxical to suggest that Yeats did not want unity, "Unity of Being," in any ultimate form.[19]

It is not only in the bland middle-class world of the first act of *Where There Is Nothing* (1903) that destruction, the "clashing of swords," is necessary; the battle must be fought everywhere, constantly, even in Heaven itself. What is the battle against except order, form, a stifling "Unity of Being" that would destroy the holy process of becoming? The Nietzschean hero of *Where There Is Nothing*, Paul Ruttlege, says:

". . . we cannot destroy the world with armies, it is inside our minds that it must be destroyed, it must be consumed in a moment inside our minds." [20]

For "where there is nothing, there is God" and, conversely—though Yeats does not state this, as Nietzsche did—"where there is God, there is nothing." In *The Unicorn From the Stars* (1908), the mystic Martin, waking from a trance, speaks of his vision of paradise:

"I have seen the shining people. . . . All that they did was but the overflowing of their idleness, and their days were a dance bred of the secret frenzy of their hearts, or a battle where the sword made a sound that was like laughter." [21]

The music of paradise is "the continual clashing of swords." Nothing must be allowed to come to rest, to reach fruition. The only fruition honored is that of death, which produces an ecstasy that comes from a sudden enlargement of vision—the breaking-down of the dykes that separate man from man—so that personality is finally lost, annihilated by violence. The changing of one's shape is both dreaded and desired, for this magical transformation signals the ultimate loss of self. In *On Baile's Strand* (1904), Cuchulain is deceived by more than one changing of shape: he cannot recognize his own son, he cannot recognize the waves that engulf him, but, more than that, he will lose his own shape, the shape of his sanity. A chorus sings of the mysterious allurement of madness:

> May this fire have driven out
> The Shape-Changers that can put
> Ruin on a great king's house
> Until all be ruinous.
> Names whereby a man has known
> The threshold and the hearthstone,
> Gather on the wind and drive
> The women none can kiss and thrive,
> For they are but whirling wind,
> Out of memory and mind.
> They would make a prince decay
> With light images of clay
> Planted in the running wave;
> Or, for many shapes they have,
> They would change them into hounds
> Until he had died of his wounds,
> Though the change were but a whim. . . .[22]

But man, like Cuchulain, must submit to this madness; he must surrender the shape of his own life, freeing his soul to flow out into nature. Passion and its necessary violence redeem and make a kind of eternity. Yeats chooses the spectacular and tradition-honored device of madness to demonstrate the precariousness of an ordered world, for chaos, rather than man's own evil, is the antithesis to various deceits of humanism. Even a more moderate form of madness, the extremes of sexual love, demonstrates the fragility of human identity, for the surrender of the ego to the erotic drives us to sing out sentences not our own—"Whence had they come," Yeats asks in the eighth of the Supernatural Songs of A *Full Moon in March,* "The hand and lash that beat down frigid Rome?" Yet the surrender of the self results in a "sacred drama" that may transform the world, in the instant of conception of a Charlemagne or a Helen or a Cuchulain.

Events of bizarre violence take place nearly everywhere in Yeats's work: the plays as "dances" are meant to convey suffering raised to a superhuman sweetness, the articulation of the emotions that accompany pain without the reality of pain itself, the Apollonian compression of Dionysian frenzy. It is only at such moments that the impersonal touches upon the personal, burning away the curse of specific character. Character is present only in comedy; in tragedy its place is taken by passions, motives, events, and moments of ritualistic violence and beauty, such an art being an "unreal" art because it faces continuously a supreme crisis.[23] The most extreme form of such loss of identity is found in the ceremonial beheading of a poet, so that he is no longer a man but his singing, his fateful words, a man reduced to the barest—and most unreal—of essences. Even the conception of some of Yeats's later works, like *The Death of Cuchulain,* with its antitheatrical opening (anticipating the comic-grotesque exaggerations of what is called the theater of the absurd, a willful and jarring self-consciousness), is an as-

160

sault upon an audience's expectations and a writer's most basic form of violent activity.

As in "Vacillation," the poet understands himself running a course between unknowable extremities, the antinomies of day and night, life and death. It is his wisest gesture to let all things pass away, but his most human gesture to make them stay and make a tragic shape out of them. The essential drama of this choice comes to no conclusion. Yeats is among the greatest of poets, not only because of his powerful and delicate sense of language but also because of his inability to make himself "pure" as a poet or a thinker, to dismiss the richness of pain and chaos for the articulation of a "Unity of Being."

7

TRAGIC RITES IN YEATS'S "A Full Moon in March"

One of the outstanding features of Yeats's poetry and plays is the obsessive commitment to a transposing of daimonic knowledge into human language. Yeats has stated that he felt his plays are "not drama but the ritual of a lost faith." [1] The human consciousness possesses something that is prior to itself and to individual existential experience; it is Yeats's sacred duty as a poet to translate the ineffable into a fable strong enough to bear the burden of this forbidden knowledge. The language used must be that of symbolism, of course, but while such language is used consciously by the magician, it can be used only half unconsciously by the magician's successors—

165

the poet, the musician, and the artist. Yeats as a playwright is all three—poet, musician, artist—drawing upon mysterious associations that are "beyond the reach of the individual 'subconscious.'" [2] As the heroes in his tragedies suffer their ordeals they are not fulfilling themselves as individuals or as representative social beings—rounding out a tragic sequence of events subsequent to a certain personal decision—but illuminating for audience and reader the archetypal experience their suffering embodies. All Yeats's plays may be called religious dramas, celebrations of a unique kind of mass.

In an unpublished dialogue, "The Poet and the Actress" (1916), Yeats talks about the process of recording a symbolic action. The art he most desires to create has a human hero, but an antagonist who is not human and who speaks in an inhuman tongue; when the emotional expressiveness of a certain situation is increased, one moves away from ordinary mimicry or the recording of facts, and the body, as if coming alive, "begins to take poses or even move in a dance. . . . Speech becomes rhythmical, full of suggestion, and as this change takes place we begin to possess, instead of the real world of the mimics, solitudes and wildernesses peopled by divinities and daimons, vast sentiments, the desires of the heart cast forth into forms, mythological beings, a frenzied parturition." [3] All such art is a journey into the interior of the race. There is no concern in Yeats, as there is in most writers, for the attempted redemption of any human life. The individual has no existence in Yeats's imagination—which seems paradoxical in the light of his intense interest in personalities and the heavily personal nature of much of his poetry—yet his question has always been, *Which of her forms has shown her substance right?* The accidental, temporal form of a human being may be a disguise of his true substance, even from himself. The only possible redemption would be a purification of this temporality. Yeats's tragic heroes are heroic because they are gifted with the audacity to undertake certain actions; though they fail, though they do not personally transcend their fates, they are heroic in their ritualistic enactment of the common human dilemma. We do battle, but battle with a shadow, a dream; we pit our human language against an inhuman language. Life may be an irrational bitterness, as Yeats says in *A Vision*, but the art that life makes possible must be both complex and simple, a presentation of timeless wisdom.

In the tragedies of Yeats one is struck by the ease with which characters assume their fates, and even by the playwright's offhand suggestion (usually introductory to the plays' actions) that the actors, the dancers, the "characters" onstage might be readily switched around. Obviously this is not realistic drama, yet it is surprising to see how totally Yeats has abandoned the most basic desire of the imagination—to be lied to in a realistic manner. Like contemporary dramatists of the absurd, Yeats refuses to sustain an illusion. He rejects without sentiment the middle-class and essentially anti-imaginative demand for verisimilitude: it is characteristic of him to find pleasure in the disruptive element of the Fool in *King Lear*, who says to the audience, "This prophecy Merlin shall make, for I live before his time." [4] Yeats's art is one of intense delicacy and intense violence, an art of the invisible movement in which one passes over into the other and then back into the first, the symbolic rhythm of his plays moving from one silence to a more profound silence. And not all of the violent activity is

167

thematic: his dramatizations are clearly meant to subject the viewer to a certain violent rearrangement of his experience as a viewer, along with the more crucial rearrangement of his experience as a human being.

Myth belongs to everyone and to no one. Poets and playwrights draw upon myths but cannot create them. Instead, they create private fantasies that may repeat or exaggerate cultural myths, and their contribution to this body of legend becomes in itself mythical, a part of the total myth. In this respect Yeats's mysticism, which is often annoying, would be substantiated by such diverse thinkers as Eliot (notably in "Tradition and the Individual Talent") and Claude Lévi-Strauss, to whom Freud's analysis of the Oedipus complex should be included among the recorded versions of the Oedipus myth, as part of its totality.[5] Yeats's compulsive desire to translate the lost faith into poetry necessitates his working with legendary and impersonal elements, his use of repetition and exaggeration and physical simplicity (especially his use of masks) having as its function the reinforcement of the archetypal structure of a myth that is previously known, or felt, by its audience. He shares these techniques with the anonymous priests and poets and storytellers who have kept such myths alive. Yeats's antagonism to science, which evidently dates back to his early youth, is a predictable aspect of his concern for "lost ritual." He is quite obviously a man who has chosen to bypass the language of science for the language of myth, and A Vision is his apology for such a choice, a purely fictional objectification of ideas that were in his mind only slightly formed until the time, or times, at which he wrote the book. He has chosen deliberately the mystical belief of cyclical history over the more modern conception of progress, for, as he says in his notes to *The Words upon the Window-Pane* (the play is dated 1934, the notes, 1931), though man's knowledge is too limited to prove either concept of history correct, "the eternal circuit may best suit our preoccupation with the soul's salvation, our individualism, our solitude." [6] His is a mythical organization of the world in which certain elements become gradually knowable:

1 The human personality is fluid, and the boundaries between personalities are fluid.

2 All that is not consciousness (even nature) is excluded.

3 Men are actors who do not simply mimic men in the "real world," but who are "acting" an eternal drama that identifies them with the eternal; therefore we are always acting, we are always actors.

4 The most powerful art is ceremonial, so that word and gesture never express spontaneous emotion, or even point toward simple referents, but *are* the essence of the ceremony itself.

5 The process of logical thought is not suspended, but is wholly transformed into the process of mythical thought, where its step-by-step inevitability prevails, but where its premises and conclusions may be fantastic.

The tragic fact of metamorphosis is at the heart of Yeats's poetry. Half consciously he seems to have chosen this primitive "logical thought" over the more commonplace and sanitary belief in the permanent isolation of human beings from one another and from the world of nature, whether animals, plants, or inanimate matter. The primitive imagination accepts totally the fact of miraculous change: what would be miraculous to them is our conception of a conclusion, an ending of spirit and energy. Such metamorphoses are not inexplicable, but are not subjected to explanations at all; indeed, the concept of an "explanation," the psychological demand for an explanation, is foreign to such thinking. The identification of hero with action, the fact of a heroic gesture *constituting* the entire history of a human being, is fundamental to the mythical world: not that one's life runs up to a certain moment in history, at which it is justified or redeemed or somehow explained, but that the moment itself has always existed, as a kind of slot that will be filled by a certain person at a certain time. Thus action and passivity are perfectly mated. Violence and stillness are one. Yeats asks his famous question in "Among School Children"—

> O chestnut-tree, great-rooted blossomer,
> Are you the leaf, the blossom or the bole?
> O body swayed to music, O brightening glance,
> How can we know the dancer from the dance?

—and the answer is that we cannot know the dancer from the dance, man from his "dance," his shadowy struggle with the other–worldly antagonist. Yeats's tragedies are rituals of sacrifice in which the human element risks his humanity for supernatural knowledge (often through the flesh, through sexual intercourse with the other–worldly), is defeated or broken, and perishes into God—which is to say, into reality. Like man, God has no personal identity; God is the sum of all that is real, all that is consciousness, the historical necessity that man has resisted. Thus the plays are rites that set up the rejection of one kind of reality in favor of another, a reality that cannot be demonstrated or experienced but can only be suggested through holy images.

Yeats's *A Full Moon in March* (1935) is one of his

most simple and most effective tragedies. Its simplicity is a risk that Yeats has taken, but not unwisely. The play succeeds through the perfection of its language and images in generating a vision through a dance; the vision (which is spiritual) arises out of the dance (which is physical, and entered into out of suffering). The play's elements are almost crudely allegorical: a Queen, a Swineherd, their mating on the night of the full moon. The play is a reworking of the less effective *The King of the Great Clock Tower*, where the King of "time" is married to the Queen of "timelessness," in that mysterious land referred to as Tir-nan-oge, where lad and lass are "bobbins where all time is bound and wound." A *Full Moon in March* begins with that peculiar sense of formlessness and sense of a drama in the making—which characterizes other plays of Yeats as well as those of Chekhov and contemporary playwrights of the absurd—a conscious straining against convention, against the completion of a perfect circle. In the first lines, one attendant says to another: "What do we do? / What part do we take? / What did he say?" One of the features of Yeats's art is the preponderance of questions without answers.

Rigorous in his adherence to the inevitability of fate, Yeats is nevertheless rebelling against the formality of this kind of art work. His is an artifice doubly disturbing because doubly imagined. *The Death of Cuchulain* (1939) begins with an introduction by a very old man "looking like something out of mythology," who states that he has been asked to produce a play called *The Death of Cuchulain*. He grows increasingly bitter and angry until he is quieted by the musicians, whereupon he explains: "I asked them to do that if I was getting excited. If you were as old you would find it easy to get

171

excited." By this technique Yeats fuses together extreme forms of realism—the admission that this is a play, that it exists in a theater with musicians (not just music), and that it will have a subject—and antirealism, the material of the play itself. Yeats's objections to the theater of Ibsen and the general naturalistic trend of modern thought are well known, but less well known are his own gestures of rebellion against the play as a single image that exists delicately in a world unrelated to history. But more than this, he seems to be breaking down the barrier between poet and audience, insisting upon the illusory aspect of this phenomenalistic art in order to impress upon his audience the greater reality, which is that his art is glorifying. Dismissing a commonplace metaphysical assumption, he jars us into seeking reality elsewhere. Language belongs to an essentially logical imagination, despite its capacity for evoking the mysterious; it is music that expresses man's relationship between himself and the community of the world. In the essay "The Tragic Theater" (1910), Yeats speaks of tragedy as "a drowning and breaking of the dykes that separate man from man" (calling to mind Nietzsche's remarks in *The Birth of Tragedy* on Apollo setting up walls between us that Dionysus breaks down); tragedy performs, therefore, a necessary act. In a similar manner the playwright himself, though committed to language, gives us the music of a work of art that establishes a certain nonlinguistic vision. The convention of the play itself must be violated, then, for it is an anticipation of the violence to be suffered by the human hero of the play. A *Full Moon in March* is probably the only play of Yeats in which music accomplishes for the dancers what language could not.

The attendants' opening questions suggest also the

formlessness of a world sluggish with winter, waiting for its magical rejuvenation by the fusion of male and female. There is indecision, a lack of purpose; no conscious choices can be made. Yet the first song of the play ("Every loutish lad in love") tells us that the play is in a sense complete: it has happened before, everything is over; this is simply a repetition of the sacrifice. The fusion of "crown of gold" and "dung of swine" is the climax of the play, the familiar Yeatsian paradox of the trapped but orderly and beautiful self seeking its regeneration in the gyres of physical life. Superhuman and human are to be mated, the "image" and the poet are to be mated, the warring poles of body and soul are to be mated by violent magic. Nietzsche's Primordial Unity will be achieved through the repetition of this sacred mass, wherein neurotic private behavior is raised to the level of a mythological incarnation.

"Neurotic private behavior" seems an extreme appraisal of the hero's actions in *A Full Moon in March*. But the implication of the Swineherd's unconscious desire for death is unmistakable: one would have to read Yeats with an obsessional interest in his allegorical representation of the Poet[7] to ignore this psychological fact. The poet is not represented by either the Queen or the Swineherd, but by a fusion of the two that takes place only to music, that is, in a kind of silence; the female sinks into her bridal sleep, with the severed head on her breast, the Swineherd, now dead, having magically impregnated her. The play ends upon this gesture, and there is no anticipation of the fruit of their union. In *The King of the Great Clock Tower*, the Queen suggests that the offspring will be unnatural, terrifying, the destruction of woman's beauty (the tumultuous occasion of the im-

173

pregnating of human women with inhuman seed is celebrated often in Yeats):

> He longs to kill
> My body, until
> That sudden shudder
> And limbs lie still.
> O, what may come
> Into my womb,
> What caterpillar
> My beauty consume?

It is possible to think of the union of image and poet as mutually destructive, then, the battle with a dream and emblematic of the impossibility of fusing opposites. Self and antiself remain eternally opposed, though eternally drawn together, like those woeful lovers Yeats is so fond of and about whom he writes in *The Dreaming of the Bones*—male and female who yearn to consummate their love but are for some reason prevented from doing so, and so are "damned." The tension of apartness produces human suffering, but the relaxation of tension, the ultimate impregnation of the symbolic Queen, produces only death once the moment of impregnation is past.

That the Swineherd desires to sing before the Queen places him in a traditional context—he is a lover who will dare obstacles in order to win a woman's love—but his sense of this mission and his enthusiasm for it are confused. He seems not to understand clearly why he has come to the Queen's court, though the traditional rewards of Queen and kingdom are mentioned. As if arousing himself into consciousness, the Swineherd assesses his life and wonders at his conception:

> But when I look into a stream, the face
> That trembles upon the surface makes me think
> My origin more foul than rag or flesh.

Given such an origin, he can know nothing of beauty and, knowing nothing, has committed a blasphemy against the Queen. She orders his head cut off. Her own face is veiled, for certainly in this work the head and face are sexually powerful images—the mouth especially, the magical place of the voice. "My face is pure," the Queen declares. "Had it but known the insult of his eyes / I had torn it with these nails." Physical beauty, the subject of so much speculation on Yeats's part,[8] is rejected by the Swineherd:

> What do those features matter? When I set out
> I picked a number on the roulette wheel.
> I trust the wheel, as every lover must.

The lover is at once the Swineherd and the lover of a God to prove terrible; he is bestial—or of an origin more foul than flesh—and at the same time a kind of saint, or at least a "martyr" to the purity of a veiled face. As the persona, Michael Robartes says in the Notes to *Calvary* that it is easy to worship God's choice, his will, but a higher worship is that of God in His chance: ". . . and that moment when I understand the immensity of His Chance is the moment when I am nearest Him." The lover must love his God or the image of God in total abandonment of human hope, relinquishing the predictability of the human world. In *The Words Upon the Window-Pane*, it is Swift's failure to give himself up to chance that constitutes his doom; when Vanessa tries to lure him into the uncertainty of love, he refuses her. She puts his hands upon her breast and says, "O, it is white—white as the gambler's dice—white ivory dice. Think of the uncertainty. Perhaps a mad child—perhaps a rascal—perhaps a knave—perhaps not, Jonathan. The dice of the intellect are loaded, but I am the common ivory dice." But Swift, a far different man from the Swineherd, cannot surrender. Consequently, he outlives everyone, dies wretchedly, and cries out at the end of Yeats's play: "Perish the day on which I was born!"

By contrast, the Swineherd is put to death immediately for his audacity in desiring the Queen. That his death is emblematic of man's need for suffering is clear, and is underlined by Yeats's reference to Christ upon the cross in the earlier, third manuscript version of the play. The Swineherd has no personality, but he shares with all men the magical power of begetting life, here upon the most distant and forbidding of virgins. He says:

> There is a story in my country of a woman
> That stood all bathed in blood—a drop of blood
> Entered her womb and there begat a child.

If one of the functions of this strange play is to rid the Swineherd of his body, another is to emphasize the extraordinarily brutal power of man's seed. The demand for life is so strong that even death cannot destroy it; the "drop of blood" is powerful enough to impregnate a woman. Yeats exaggerates the nightmarish power of sex at the same time that he rids the Swineherd of his body, and it is an ironic fact that the severed head, singing, at last purified of the rag and flesh and transformed totally into music, is vividly potent. Only at this time can the head, held high in the air by the blood-smeared hands of the Queen, display its power. The woman has brought about the man's castration, and it is a castration the man has, for some reason, desired. Yeats believes that the equation of sex and music is stronger than the equation of sex and the flesh, and that the highest display of sex is in the form of music, or of poetry; this alone has the power to impregnate the virginal image.

Frank Kermode has devoted an entire book, *The Romantic Image*, to a study of the various forms of the dancer—the female who is all movement and yet essentially still, without personality, who represents timelessness, the spirit, the mystery of Byzantium and its golden art. "The Stroller is the Artist and the Queen is the Image, out of time and deathless, speaking no intellectual language," [9] Kermode says in reference to *The King of the Great Clock Tower*, but this holds true for *A Full Moon in March* as well. But there is more to the Salomé-figure than her Platonic cruelty. She is also a collaborator in the making of a poem, the means by which the human transcends himself. If the Swineherd is a kind of bestial Christ, like Crazy Jane willing to descend into the hellish joy of physical life, the Queen is a kind of Christ, a supernatural being whose actual body will be violated, sacrificed so that something will be born out of it. In the prologue to *The Death of Cuchulain*, the Old Man says, "Emer must dance, there must be severed heads—I am old, I belong to mythology—severed heads for her to dance before." Why must there be severed heads for the female to dance before? Scattered throughout Yeats's writings are odd references to the mutilation of men through the command of women, including a bizarre little anecdote in "The Tower" where a servingman brings a wealthy woman, Mrs. French, the ears of an insolent farmer "in a little covered dish." In Yeats's last play, the

177

woman, Emer, faithful wife of Cuchulain, is no traditional Salomé-figure, though she dances before the heads
of those who have wounded her husband and before his
head, which may be raised above the others according to
Yeats's stage directions. So the husband's head has domi-
nance over the rest of the stage. Emer has not caused
Cuchulain to be beheaded, but her presence seems to be
necessary, in Yeats's imagination, in order that he become transformed into his ultimate shape. She is, like the
winter Queen of A *Full Moon in March*, a savior who
dances in "adoration or triumph," surrendering herself to
the head:

> She is about to prostrate herself before it, perhaps does so,
> then rises, looking up as if listening. . . . There is silence,
> and in the silence a few faint bird notes.

Thus, Cuchulain is transformed; he is saved, immortal-
ized in the music of the "few faint bird notes."

In D. H. Lawrence's *Women in Love*, which Yeats
read with enthusiasm, there are two totemic images
(these are actual works of art) that unsettle or "annihi-
late" the intellect. One is a carved figure of an African
woman in labor. Seeing it, Gerald, who will be destroyed
by a woman whom he loves, thinks that it is a "terrible"
thing, "abstracted in utter physical stress." He resents it;
he is shocked that it is called art, for to him the woman's
face is "abstracted almost into meaninglessness by the
weight of sensation beneath." [10] Willful as Gerald, and
also destined to be defeated, is the strange Hermione,
who wants to extract from Birkin the "secret" of his
being. She watches him copying a picture of geese, and
her curiosity about his interest in it leads him to tell her:
"I know what centers they live from—what they perceive

178

and feel—the hot, stinging centrality of a goose in the flux of cold water and mud—the curious bitter stinging heat of a goose's blood, entering their own blood like an inoculation of corruptive fire—fire of the cold-burning mud—the lotus mystery." Hermione is extremely shaken by this, witless, decentralized. She suffers "the ghastliness of dissolution"; she is attacked beneath his words with "some insidious occult potency." [11] The image is both artificial and vital; it contains life within itself, but a "decentralized" life, not of the intellect or the will, but of a supreme sensuality that is the ultimate holiness. The will of man must perish into such sensuality in order to be born again.

A *Full Moon in March* explores the ghastliness of this dissolution in the most barren of terms. The play is about the gestures that constitute a tragic action, not about people who are involved in a tragic action. By abandoning nearly all the restrictions of realism, Yeats is able to give us the tragic essence of human strife—the drawing of the human out of itself, into the sphere of the inhuman, which for Yeats demands the death of the body. No existentialist, Yeats is clearly able to believe that the death of the body, and its mutilation, does in some way free the spirit, or exaggerate and emphasize the spirit, so that impurities are lost. His fascination with the concept of "dreaming-back," of reliving certain events in one's past life again and again in order to be purged of them, his fascination with the whole idea of the eternal recurrence, suggests that in his imagination life itself may attain the purity of a ritual. It is not simply Yeats's dramatic work that is the "ritual" of a lost faith, but the fact of personality, of existence itself. We dream back endlessly until, having found our antithesis in the form of a castrating and beautiful dancer, we are released from time and made immortal. (So in dreams, as Freud points out, the dreamer goes back again and again to disquieting memories in order to master them, to purge them finally.) For the soul, despite its agonies, is perpetually virginal; Yeats says in A Vision that "the tragedy of sexual intercourse is the perpetual virginity of the soul." [12] How to desecrate this perpetual virginity?—how to break loose from the tragedy of the body? His plays are rites, with stories built around them, meant to demonstrate the way back out of our human predicament.

At the same time, the neurotic desire of the Swineherd-as-male to be castrated at the hands of the Queen points out a tragic flaw in the composition of human passions. Passionate love, Yeats says in A Vision, "is from the Daimon which seeks by union with some other Daimon to reconstruct above the antinomies its own nature." [13] But the fulfillment of the highest passion—sexual passion— must be at the moment of death, so that passion itself becomes not life-giving or life-enhancing but, in Nietzsche's terms, one of the many "destroyers of the body." For Nietzsche, passion is complex, but this particular kind of passion is good; for Yeats, the surrender to the bloody mystery is a terrible thing, whether it is necessary or not. And so it is in Yeats's imagination that Christ is associated with Dionysus, while to Nietzsche (and to most of us) Dionysus is opposed eternally to Christ as a savior, the two of them being imagined in a perpetual struggle for men's souls. When Christ walks across the room in The Resurrection, he is a vision of terror. He is not Apollonian, not a builder of walls between people, but the apocalyptic means by which the walls of rationality are torn down "at the moment when knowledge and order seems complete. . . ." It is always at this moment, of course, that the monster stirs. So it would be no surprise to discover that Yeats equates the celibate Christ with the unruliness of sexual passion as well. Christ's coming initiates the death of man, man's dying into God and into a terrible, irresistible reality. The Swineherd is a type of Christ, at the same time that the Queen, in her frigid holiness, is a kind of God, an external reality that draws men into it and into death.

This dramatization of the movement of man into something totally outside himself, of the loss of physical and subjective determination, suggests a concern with the tragedy of history as well. For just as the proudly masculine Swineherd desires his castration and the death of his masculinity, so does an entire civilization desire its sacrificial death at the hands of a god. Yeats demonstrates in his tragedies the moment at which man moves "out" of himself, out of the last phase of subjectivity; he is killed and therefore born into a new phase, that of objectivity; the neurotic desire for an apocalyptic close to one era is signaled by a willingness to equate physical death and music, the highest of the arts. Though beautiful, it is a decadent music; it is the music of our dying era. As in "The Statues," one of Yeats's last poems, we will give to the characterless beauty of the winter Queen our own character, our personality, our blood, bringing human passion to the inhuman by pressing live lips upon "a plummet-measured face." Like Schopenhauer and Mann—though unlike Nietzsche—Yeats naturally associates death and music. (For Schopenhauer, man's escape from the will is through either art or death, and the highest of the arts is music. The female, who seduces man into reproducing and continuing the species—with its misery—is an ally of the will, the unconscious.) Thus art is a transcendence of time, but it is also a suicidal gesture. One action dies continually into another, one kind of life feeding another: "Love's pleasure drives his love away,/ The painter's brush consumes his dreams." As with the artist, the most intense of human beings, so the entire subjective gyre must die into its antithesis. This is most clearly demonstrated in the peculiar *The Player Queen* (1922), where the Poet is abandoned by his wife, who is set up as a surrogate queen, a "muse," and the entire kingdom seems to be awaiting the advent of a "new dispensation" in the coming of the Unicorn— that chaste, white, violent beast from the stars.

The anticipation of the coming of a new beast, a beast-deity with powers drawn from its blank, pitiless chastity, is paralleled by the very structure of most of Yeats's plays. Yeats imagines dream-worlds analogous to his idea of contemporary history and populates them with abstractions of men, who act out formula-like rites of sacrifice. This motif is sounded as early as *The Countess Cathleen*, and other early, minor plays turn upon a revelation of one kind or another, an illumination of the "unknown language." These plays can be called "miracle" plays. The violent fact of miracle is usually signaled by a metamorphosis (as in *A Full Moon in March*, where a man becomes a song, and in *The Herne's Egg*, where a man becomes a donkey) or by the appearance of a spectacle that denies sane expectations (the walking of Christ across the room in *The Resurrection*; the return of the hoofbeats in *Purgatory*), which is, perhaps, only another kind of metamorphosis, a denial of the permanent boundaries between personalities that signals the end of one era and the start of another.

Like *A Full Moon in March, At the Hawk's Well*
(1917) and *The Death of Cuchulain* (1939) deal with
the confrontation of a human hero and an inhuman antagonist. The mystery is in the antagonist's need for a
human counterpart. The Hawk-Woman, "the unappeas-
able shadow," dances apparently in a kind of unconscious
state, as if doomed to repeat an action she cannot understand. She belongs to mythology. Being female, she is the
antithesis of the young hero Cuchulain (just as Cuchulain in his energetic youth is the antithesis of the Old
Man); she is the Woman of the Sidhe who continually
lures men out from the boundaries of their worlds and
destroys them. Her hawk cry, like the apparent madness
of the Queen in *A Full Moon in March*, is not in her
control: "It was her mouth, and yet not she, that cried./
It was the shadow cried behind her mouth." She is "possessed": "Who knows whom she will murder or betray/
Before she awakes in ignorance of it all,/ And gathers up
the leaves?" The Dancer, whether goddess or muse or
both, performs her role in the ritual with no more autonomy than the human protagonist. In *The Only Jealousy
of Emer* (1919), the same woman dances again for Cuchulain, explaining her fate: "Because I long I am not
complete." According to Yeats's stage directions, she is
to be costumed so as to suggest an idol, and her lines
make clear the temptation she represents for the artist
locked in time and mortality:

> Then kiss my mouth. Though memory
> Be beauty's bitterest enemy
> I have no dread, for at my kiss
> Memory on the moment vanishes;
> Nothing but beauty can remain.
>
> .   .   .   .

Time shall seem to stay his course;
When your mouth and my mouth meet
All my round shall be complete
Imagining all its circles run;
And there shall be oblivion
Even to quench Cuchulain's drouth,
Even to still that heart.

But the faithfulness of Emer prevents Cuchulain's transformation, and he returns to life, just as, in *At the Hawk's Well,* his desire for this very knowledge costs him the immortality the well's water is said to contain. *The Death of Cuchulain,* Yeats's last play, is a striking work in which the various themes of his other tragedies are sounded once more, and the introduction and finish —the Old Man and the Street-Singers—make the work seem nearly contemporary. The bareness of the stage suggests the bareness of a dream, as in *Purgatory,* which will be populated by figures out of the Old Man's imagination. He has sought out the tragic dancer, upon whose neck "love and loathing, life and death" hang, for he despises the modern world. "I spit! I spit! I spit!" he cries, and the stage darkens so that we may witness a dream-spectacle worthy of the Old Man's respect.

Cuchulain's death does not come from any noble source, but from the degraded Blind Man (he is from *On Baile's Strand,* but his clever "objective" personality suggests as well the blind man of *The Cat and the Moon*). The play's several confrontations represent a "dreaming-back" of the hero in terms of the women in his life, women who are mythical and deadly and yet ultimately powerless to destroy him. The Dancer does not destroy the tragic hero, for she is his means of fulfillment and he hers; he is destroyed instead by the vulgarity of the Blind

184

Man, which is to say the vulgarity of the New Dispensation, the "excrement" that Locke gave back when he took away the living world.[14] Cuchulain is man as Yeats imagines him in our era, faced with the squalid violence of a modern Ireland or a modern Europe. No "evil" exists in Yeats, so far as I can determine, but the function of dramatic evil is taken over by the fact of chaos, personal and historical. Yeats's dismissal of Whitman because he lacked a sense of evil is explicable, then—the Nietzschean transcendence of good and evil being threatened by what is for Zarathustra the "Ugliest Man" and what is for Yeats the filth of a modern civilization.

In the notes to *The Cat and the Moon*, Yeats says:

> Perhaps some early Christian . . . thought as I do, saw in the changes of the moon all the cycles: the soul realising its separate being in the full moon, then, as the moon seems to approach the sun and dwindle away, all but realising its absorption in God, only to whirl away once more: the mind of a man, separating itself from the common matrix . . . through struggle . . . to roundness, completeness, and then externalising, intellectualising, systematising, until at last it lies dead, a spider smothered in its own web.[15]

The music at the conclusion of *The Death of Cuchulain* is modern and loud, the music of an Irish fair. A Street-Singer sings these cryptic words:

> No body like his body
> Has modern woman borne,
> But an old man looking on life
> Imagines it in scorn.

If the Old Man, who speaks for Yeats, looks upon modern bodies with scorn, this is understandable; but if the words are read in another way, it would seem that the

185

Old Man views even Cuchulain and his ancient race with scorn, for "centuries have passed/ Since they were living men."

Like Chekhov, Yeats is concerned with the disintegration of a culture, but he is impatient with the furniture that makes up this culture; for him everything must be reduced to purity, pure act. Chekhov's gentle tragedies are demonstrations of chaos and might be used to further illustrate the doom of Yeats's subjective gyre—the nightmare of Phase 23, our era, where men are fascinated by the external world for its own sake, and causation and sequence are denied. This new era levels personality, a "deluge of experience" breaks over us and within us, destroying limits; man is "no hard bright mirror dawdling by the dry sticks of a hedge, but a swimmer, or rather the waves themselves. In this new literature . . . man in himself is nothing." [16] In these final convulsions, the intellect can no longer rule itself; it is defeated by the ghosts of its own sleep. That profound question of *The Words upon the Window-Pane*, "Was Swift mad? Or was it the intellect itself that was mad?" is one of Yeats's many questions about knowledge and power, but the answer is "Yes," it is the intellect itself that is mad, and the answer is "No," Leda cannot "put on his knowledge with his power."

As in his poetry, Yeats discovers in his plays that the philosophic desire for permanence is not compatible with the evidence of the senses. His plays become increasingly ironic and bitter as he charts the fate of the doomed individual in a historical phase in which individuals can no longer survive. Yeats's best poetry shows that he is the kind of poet to whom dramatic tensions come naturally, and to whom a desire for unity is at best a working antithesis to the fact of change. What remains in his art is emotion, the "purity" of emotion. In the notes to *The Only Jealousy of Emer,* Yeats denounces the modern "Lockian" world and states, "All emotion seeks the unconditioned, the pure act of Berkeley and Aquinas . . ." [17] Much earlier, in the essay "The Emotion of Multitude" (1903), he remarks that *Lear* is less the history of one man than the history of a whole evil time, the world being imagined through shadow beyond shadow, the father Gloucester beyond the father Lear, until an entire historical epoch is encompassed. The highest of tragic works draw us out of our epochs, which are likely to be squalid; like the magical dancers of Yeats's plays, such art entices us beyond our limitations. There is not so much emphasis upon "tragic joy" in the plays as there is in certain of Yeats's poetry, but the possibility is still held out to us of a metamorphosis through art, a changing of the filthy general fate into the mythological immortality of the artist. For while the tragic relationship of self and fate cannot be resolved, the transcendence of the self—even through death and mutilation—may bring about a higher, more permanent condition. Is Cuchulain's dignity honored or parodied by the Street-Singer's song? Is "desecration and the lover's night" a profound enough experience to justify death? The "pitchers" that carry "all time's completed treasure" are tight as a woman's frigid and unloving body, as the singers in *A Full Moon in March* say, and their violation signals the surrender of one kind of self so that another may be born.

8

ART AT THE EDGE OF IMPOSSIBILITY: Mann's "Dr. Faustus"

He shall be the greatest who can be the loneliest, the most hidden, the most deviating, the human being beyond good and evil, the master of his virtues, he that is overrich in will.

Nietzsche,
Beyond Good and Evil [1]

A Faustian claim: the language of passion, of hubris and tragedy, a truly German secularization of religious quest and saviordom, the statement is typically Nietzsche, and it is echoed in other Nietzschean claims of a unique destiny: "Posthumous men—I, for example—are understood worse than timely ones, but *heard* better. More precisely, we are never understood—*hence* our authority." [2]

When the Devil appears in *Dr. Faustus* to speak to the doomed genius, Adrian Leverkühn, he commends Adrian for having undertaken his peculiar destiny, for wanting to give away his soul in order to compose music for the future. It will be guaranteed to Adrian:

". . . not only that toward the end of your houre-glasse years your sense of your power and splendour will more and more outweigh [your disease] and finally mount to most triumphant well-being, to a sense of bursting health, to the walk and way of a god. That is only the subjective side of the thing. . . . Know, then, we pledge you the success of that which with our help you will accomplish. You will lead the way, you will strike up the march of the future, the lads will swear by your name, who thanks to your madness will no longer need to be mad. . . . Not only will you break through the paralyzing difficulties of the time—you will break through time itself, by which I mean the cultural epoch and its cult, and dare to be barbaric, twice barbaric indeed. . . ." [3]

What is the meaning of "breaking through"? What is the destiny of these posthumous men, who are indeed never quite understood and who seem with a melancholy genius to have understood themselves so thoroughly? Adrian is not Nietzsche; but Nietzsche is the basis for much of Adrian's personality, his life, his terrible fate (years of infantile madness), even the sordid circumstances leading to this fate (syphilitic infection). Like Nietzsche, Adrian lives apart from humanity in a kind of ascetic exile; like Nietzsche, he is mocked and hated for his "barbaric" music, and gravely admired by a few who sympathize without fully understanding. In their tragic isolation—the insularity of self that praises the elemental and barbaric while having no access to it—they comprise the most extreme predicament of intellectual and artistic man. Having taken the place of the classical tragic figure —a man of nobility beset by the gods, or fate—these figures of contemporary tragedy contain their doom in themselves. It is their doom that assures their genius, their being not living men but somehow "posthumous men." They create themselves. They are beyond good and evil just as their nineteenth-century universe is speeding headlong beyond good and evil, but unknowingly, they are committed to willful ambiguity, to physical pain and deprivation that are miraculously transformed into works of genius. It will be objected to that Adrian and Nietzsche are being discussed casually as tragic figures. Clearly, one is a fictional creation and the other is a "real" person, but never has a fictional character been given such meticulously detailed evidence of his having lived and created works of art, and rarely has a "real" human being so mythologized himself. By the time of Nietzsche's madness he has become Antichrist himself, the Dionysian savior of the new, anguished world, the psychologist and poet of the future, he who glorifies the will even when it leads to nothingness. The tragedy of Adrian is similarly the tragedy of will: an egoism that seeks to control the base drives of the unconscious, an intellectuality so total that it can find no worthy objects beyond itself except shapes to be parodied, a sense of being a "firstling and premature birth of the coming century. . . ."[4]

Dr. Faustus, along with *The Magic Mountain* and *Ulysses*, is one of the most complex novels ever written. Mann's extraordinary mind leaves nothing out, resists no opportunity to analyze works of music that do not exist, misses no ironic connection between Adrian and Nietzsche, Adrian and Adam, Adrian and Germany, Adrian and "bourgeois humanism," Adrian and his prototype, Faust, who somehow incorporates in himself his tempter and seducer, the Devil. One of the highest products of

what Mann calls the reflective-analytic art, *Dr. Faustus*
repays many readings and in its ingenious artlessness
forces the reader to become a creator himself, a kind of
secondary novelist. The artlessness is a result of Mann's
technique, which presents us with the long biography of
Adrian Leverkühn that is written, or is in the process of
being written, by his old associate and admirer, Serenus
Zeitblom, Ph.D. Zeitblom has no pretensions to art; if he
seems to be respecting form and symbolism, it is not because he is "creating" but rather because he is "recording." Zeitblom may, then, quite seriously ask: "For a
man who is not an artist the question is intriguing: how
serious is the artist in what ought to be . . . his most
pressing and earnest concern; how seriously does he take
himself in it, and how much tired disillusionment, affec-
tation, flippant sense of the ridiculous is at work?" (p.
373). Mann, at an ironic distance, invites us to ponder
the "seriousness" of his Faustian parable. There is a great
deal of the "ridiculous" in it—the constant pairing-off of
characters, a kind of maniacal parody of Mann's own
penchant for the dialectical process—and the very choice
of subject matter demands that one think of other
Fausts, particularly of Goethe's Faust, and that one
make careful comparisons with the hallucinatory devil of
Ivan's intellect in *The Brothers Karamazov*. *Dr. Faustus*
exists as one of those apparently terminal works, terminal
in a genre, that operates on the verge of self-parody, of an
extreme and startling self-consciousness unthinkable in
naive art, very nearly one with the composition of Adrian's that is a "tense, neck-breaking game played by art on
the edge of impossibility" (p. 218). We are told by
Adrian himself that music and speech belong together

and are at bottom the same; language is music, music is language. And music, as the most intellectual of the arts, demands its incorporation into this most intellectual of literary modes. "This is no novel," Zeitblom explains, "in whose composition the author reveals the hearts of his characters indirectly, in the action he portrays" (p. 295). This is true, for all action is predetermined; instead, it is "being" that arrests our attention. But the work is a novel, a highly experimental novel cast in the form of a traditional critical biography, the oldest novelistic device for securing a skeptical audience's interest.

Any analysis of *Dr. Faustus* must distort the novel's complexities and subtleties. What is delicate as a strain of music must in criticism be underscored; what is symbolic, perhaps achieving its magical power on an unconscious level, must be wrenched into consciousness and connected with other symbols in the work. Symbolism exposed is no longer symbolic in the powerful sense in which Mann intends it to be: not as conscious contrivance, a linking-together of times and themes, but as the unconscious manifestation of destiny, of the mystery of a universe in which nothing is accidental. Mann's strange belief in the power of will accounts for mystifying elements in his novels; it is not to be confused with the desire for a well-written novel whose parts add up to a whole. Indeed, Mann says in his essay, "Freud and the Future," that the "apparently objective and accidental is a matter of the soul's own contriving." [5]

The question of Mann's formal technique is closely related to the question of the meaning of *Dr. Faustus*, for it is out of the apparently accidental meshing of fateful events that the tragedy of will arises—the fulfillment of violent life at the edge of the impossibility of life itself, the point at which life passes over, as Nietzsche's did, into fiction.

A Tale "Neither Short Nor Long, But Hermetic"

Mann's technique in *Dr. Faustus* consists of the layering of experience in concentric circles, rather like circles of hell. What happens once will happen again, and perhaps a third time; it is fated to recur. Nietzsche's mystical conception of the "eternal recurrence" is evoked with a vengeance in Mann's diabolical imagination, as the eternal egoism of Adrian comes to rest ultimately in the most egoistic of all conditions, infantilism, while Adrian's "soul"—that is, Adrian's music, the herald of the twice-barbaric future—is promised to us in the aftermath of the decline of individual worth. Hence the classical rise and fall of the tragic hero who subsides in the mindlessness from which he came—a true turning of the wheel of fortune, bitterly ironic. As Mann says of *The Magic Mountain*, the novel is "hermetic"—turning endlessly upon itself, complex and dazzling in its intricacy, representing by its very nearly atrophied difficulty the plight of the decadent bourgeois society with which it deals.

Dr. Faustus is subtitled "The Life of the German Composer Adrian Leverkühn as Told By a Friend." Eighteenth-century in its insistence upon biographical realism, it is also classical in its back-stepping evocation of Dante:

"The day was departing, and the brown air taking the animals, that are on earth, from their toils; and I, one alone was preparing myself to bear the war both of the journey and the pity, which memory, that errs not, shall relate. O Muses, O high Genius, now help me! O Memory, that hast inscribed what I saw, here will be shown thy nobleness." [6]

It is Zeitblom asking for aid here, Mann/Zeitblom asking the Muses for help in his creation of Mann/Leverkühn. Mann's splitting of his impulses toward bourgeois kindliness and order, and toward "barbaric" simplicity and violence, has been anticipated in his earlier works concerning artists: the melancholy yearning of Tonio Kröger for the blond, blue-eyed mediocrities forever beyond the range of his art, the violent yearning of Aschenbach for the beauties of sensual passion embodied in a spoiled Polish child. The story is Adrian's, but from Adrian's point of view there would be no story at all. His "tragedy" takes form only from the point of view of the observer, Zeitblom, who is a representative of ours, and who insists at once upon a dialectical split between types of art (pure and "impure" or acquired) and types of human beings (the ordinary man and the artist). Adrian hates the words "art" and "artist" and "inspiration" excessively; his aristocratic nihilism judges such bourgeois attempts at interpretation and classification as absurd.

In his early essay on Goethe's *Faust*, Mann remarks of Faust's desire for the synthesis of his conflicting impulses toward sensuality and spirituality that it is "half-hypocritical"; "for well he knows that dualism is the soil and the mystery of creative fruitfulness." [7] The ceaseless struggle between man's earthliness and his heavenly aspirations accounts for man himself. Furthermore, it is logical to extend this essentially Schopenhauerian dualism to the clinical Freudian dualism of id and ego—the domain of the "other," the primitive, elemental, and unconscious, and the domain of the personal, the thinking, the ever-conscious. The ego, according to Freud and Mann, does not exist in itself but as the result of violent struggles between the demanding id and the indifference of the world, its restrictions and suppressions becoming partly internalized in that mysterious part of the unconscious to which Freud gives the name "super-ego." All this is to anticipate Mann's conception of the "will," but it is necessary to note at this point the essential split in his imagination, a faith in the restless swerving from pole to pole that has its external and formal manifestation in the series of doubles (whether characters, things, or events) that make up much of the novel's substance.

The basis of the novel is a split in the psychological potentialities of man as an abstract essence—a device freely and successfully used by Conrad, Melville, and Dostoevski, among others. Therefore, Adrian is released so that he may drift to the farthest boundaries of the human, restrained by nothing: like Conrad's Kurtz, he has nothing above or below him, having "kicked himself free of the earth"; like Ahab, he dares the very fabric of the universe, which Melville has told us early in *Moby Dick* is simultaneously the fabric of his own soul; like the bizarre Karamazov family, he acts out aggression on various levels of consciousness, an aggression that finds its ultimate object in the destruction of the highest and most sensitively developed person in the novel. And Zeitblom, who worries about losing weight during the social chaos following World War I, who loves his wife exceedingly and is faithful to her, yet, in true middle-class hypocritical fashion, has experimented with a working-class "creature" whom he blithely abandons—Zeitblom remains fixed, predictable, an absolute in a world gone mad, rather prim and prudent and anti-Nazi, but unable to resist enthusiasm for such humanistic devices as German-developed torpedoes, though of course he is resolutely opposed to the war and German nationalism. Zeitblom, then, is the ordinary man writ large.

The hermetic universe begins at once, though only later in Adrian's life is the symbolic meaning made clear. He and Zeitblom grow up in a truly Edenic countryside, complete with a height called "certainly from old days and most inappropriately, Mount Zion" (p. 25). The various components of his childhood are repeated at the end of his life, in a similar Edenic setting into which he has withdrawn in a monastic, compulsive asceticism, living only in order to create music. Here he has a surrogate mother, Frau Schweigestill (whom he will call *Mutter* and *Sie* in his madness), who at first stands in for and then accompanies his real mother (*Mutter* and *Du*). Eerily, everything returns from his childhood, and yet Adrian himself is not aware, or is only half aware, of the coincidences. Zeitblom remarks: "This choice of a place to live, reproducing the earliest one, this burying of oneself in one's earliest, outlived childhood, or at least in the circumstances of the same—it might indicate attachment, but in any case it is psychologically disturbing" (p. 26). Because, in Mann, there is usually an uncanny correspondence between inner logic and outer event, it is no surprise that "at the same age, seventy-five years and strange to say almost on the same day, Max Schweigestill and Jonathan Leverkühn departed this life: the father and proprietor of Adrian's Bavarian asylum and home, and his own father up in Buchel" (p. 455). There are other doubles: the dogs Suso and Kaschperl (dogs of earthly hell in the guise of paradise, who can hear the whistle Adrian makes and who respond to it); the stable girl of childhood who teaches him songs, and the stable girl Waltpurgis. But Adrian synthesizes the two times by remarking sardonically that he incorporates in himself the elements of his earlier life. With Mephistophelian wit he states, "Where I am, there is Kaisersaschern" (p. 226). Not simply psychological, this insight is mythical as well—for Adrian senses himself as typical, a type, a dehumanized person who must fulfill his destiny as if consciously acting out a role.

In the essay on Goethe's *Faust*, Mann gives us a brief background to the Faust legends. Out of the mysterious depths of early Christian history comes the figure of Simon from Samaria, held in abhorrence by the Fathers of the Church because he founded a heretical sect, the Simonians, pretended divinity, and took about with him a woman he called Helena. All this, Mann tells us, is "mythological hocus-pocus," but it fascinates him, perhaps because it anticipates the theory of the individual-passing-into-myth that is the basis of the composition of *Joseph and his Brothers* (discussed at length in "Freud and the Future"). Simon and Helena are impostors who survive in a novel of the early Christian age called *Recognitiones*, and it is in this book that Simon becomes Faust, taking on the name "Faust." Centuries later, in 1526, a man named Georg Helmstätter sets himself in motion as the successor to this early Faust, even passing out name cards; he conforms to the original pattern by acquiring a female accomplice whom he names Helena. Fifty years after his death the first Faust-book is composed, in Frankfurt, in honor of his "miracles."

And so it came about that Helena, of antiquity, is matched with the figure of Faustus. This combination,

Mann says, "is one of those pregnant inventions that can make a period of two thousand years seem like a single span of human life." [8] And in this essay written many years before the writing of *Dr. Faustus*, Mann uses the specific term *hetaera* in connection with Helena.

All this history is interesting for its own sake, and it certainly fascinates Mann, who is already moving from the individualistic psychology of Freud to what can only be called a Jungian sense of archetypal experience—the "collective unconscious" of famed unintelligibility. But it is interesting to note that the *hetaera* appears early in Adrian's childhood, not as a woman but as an insect called to Adrian's attention by the investigations of his father, Jonathan, a good man of a typically German nature though afflicted with migraine headaches, with a "taste for research" that, according to Zeitblom, always leaned in a certain direction—"namely, the mystical or an intuitive half-mystical . . . all this had quite close relations with witchcraft" (p.17). One butterfly in Father Leverkühn's book is the *Hetera esmeralda*, an insect of transparent nudity, with only dark spots on her wings. Adrian, who forgets nothing and is sardonically quick to note a chilling relationship between various stages of his life, thinks of the diseased harlot who gives him syphilis as *Hetera esmeralda* and even dedicates a piece of music to her. But it is not only the fateful harlot who is summoned up in disguised form by Adrian's father; the condition of Adrian's very soul is suggested by the discourse on ice crystals, which vainly imitate the vegetable world of ferns and grasses and flowers, but which do not live ("To the utmost of their icy ability they dabbled in the organic" (p. 18).) [9] And the agents of syphilis itself, years later embarked upon a journey to Adrian's brain, are anticipated in the culture Jonathan Leverkühn grows in a jar, a "confused vegetation of . . . shoots . . . entirely inorganic in their origin." Through the process of osmotic pressure this crop of pseudo-plants springs forth in imitation of life, yearning for warmth and joy, but "even so they are dead," as Jonathan says, thus reducing his unsentimental son Adrian to laughter and thus anticipating the Devil's remark. Years later, when Adrian comes to understand his predicament, he says to the Devil with a casual dignity that he is being visited by an annunciation: "I am to grow osmotic growths" (p. 242). So, slowly and inevitably, the circles close about Adrian; the drama of a free soul, the embodiment of Nietzsche's ideal of man beyond good and evil, turns bitterly ironic by the process of Mann's intricate hermetic technique.

In chapter 6, when one is introduced to the rather sinister town of Kaisersaschern, the analogies between the microcosmic world of Adrian and the larger world of significance take shape. For now, reaching beyond the limitations of childhood, we discover a phenomenon: the retention in Kaisersaschern of barbarism simultaneous with the glory of European bourgeois humanism. The roots of Adrian's childhood are in the barbaric, though he is not consciously involved in it. Kaisersaschern (clearly Mann's home town of Lübeck) has a medieval air about it. Its "stamp of old-world, underground neurosis" betrays itself by the many peculiar people who live there, eccentrics and harmlessly half-mad folk. The age itself (and Zeitblom is writing this book during the rise of Hitler) "tends . . . to return to those earlier epochs; it enthusiastically re-enacts symbolic deeds of sinister significance, deeds that strike in the face the spirit of the modern age" (p. 37). Zeitblom, committed to the ego-oriented world of humanism, frightened by the very concept of the "folk," for there is something anachronistic and evil about it, "this old, folkish layer [that] survives in us all." He does not believe that the institution of religion is sufficient to restrain the passion of the "folk"; "for that, literature alone avails, humanistic science, the ideal of the free and beautiful human being." [10]

In this town, in the strange warehouse of Adrian's uncle, there is a universe of musical instruments, described with leisurely meticulousness by Mann. In this "silent paradise" that so fascinates Adrian, everything is present, every instrument except the piano. Gravitated toward music, Adrian exhibits precocity not only in his skill but in his philosophical grasp of music. Hardly more than a child, he replies to his friend Zeitblom's belief in the condition of life as necessarily residing in "belief in absolute values" with the statement, while playing the harmonium, that *relationship is everything.* "And if you want to give it a more precise name, it is ambiguity" (p. 47). A "double" of Adrian's, a famous predecessor, is summoned up in the form of Beethoven; an anecdote is told about the composer, surprised in a kind of maniacal creativity and only arbitrarily related to the world of ordinary men when friends unexpectedly visit him. It is Beethoven's Ninth Symphony that will be the ghostly double for Adrian's last work, "The Lamentation of Dr. Faustus," the ending of which has a choral part that is the reverse of the "Ode to Joy," the "negative, equally a work of genius, of that transition of the symphony into vocal jubilation" (p. 490). Mann says of Beethoven:

[His] art had overgrown itself, risen out of the habitable regions of tradition, even before the startled gaze of human eyes, into spheres of the entirely and utterly and nothing-

but personal—an ego painfully isolated in the absolute, isolated too from sense by the loss of his hearing; lonely prince
of a realm of spirits. . . . (p. 52)

As with Beethoven, so with Adrian.

Adrian's sudden desire to study theology, which he admits later is due to his desire to study demonology, brings
us into the bizarre world of Halle, medieval spiritually as
Kaisersaschern is medieval emotionally. Zeitblom dwells
uneasily upon the opposition between theology and humanism. It seems paradoxical that theology is constantly
passing over into demonology; but, obsessed as it is with
ecclesiastical brawls, self-laceration, and the "inward
and given psychological fact" that is so far removed from
philosophy, it is in danger by its very nature of becoming
demonology (p. 90).

This paradox is borne out by the ludicrous professors,
Kumpf and Schleppfuss, the one on rowdy, folksy, bawdy
terms with the "Divil," the other apparently a manifestation of the Devil himself!—for Privat-docent Schleppfuss, after lecturing for two semesters at Halle, "disappeared from the scene, I know not wither" (p. 99). In his
disturbing, rather sinister lectures, Schleppfuss seeks to
incorporate the hellish in the divine, declaring the vicious to be a part of the holy and the holy a constant
satanic temptation to violation; his Manicheanism has a
sound, though obscene, basis in the psychology of the
erotic/religious. Fond of saying "your humble servant,"
he is reincarnated later when, in Leipzig, a sly porter
leads the chaste Adrian to a house of prostitution and
thereby brings about his fall.

Adrian's strange longing for the harlot who brushes his
cheek with her arm is explained in terms of a love that is

madness. Zeitblom sees Adrian's willful possession of her diseased body as a compulsion to combine the punishment in the sin, a "mysterious longing for daemonic conception" (p. 155). Adrian seeks her out in a hospital and insists upon consummating his desire for her, though she warns him of her disease; such an act, under such circumstances, can indicate nothing but a morbid yearning for the very extremes of experience, the communion with disease, with darkness, with the unknown that Mann sees as necessary in order that great art be created. The Devil asks Adrian rhetorically whether he thinks that "any important work was ever wrought except its maker learned to understand the way of the criminal and the madman" (p. 236). It is unfortunate that Mann conceives of the harlot in abstract terms and that he does not give to this anonymous Helena any of the voluptuousness and intelligence of that other diseased temptress, Clavdia of *The Magic Mountain*. Hardly realized for us, not at all dramatized, she is little more than a projection of Adrian's desire for a communion with the unknown and the forbidden, which will unlock his creative powers but ultimately destroy him.

Comically following this episode is the mysterious encounter with the two doctors, Erasmi and Zimbalist, who are sought out to cure Adrian of his disease. But the first doctor dies suddenly, and the second doctor is arrested and taken away just as Adrian is climbing the stairs to his office—perhaps arrested by the Devil's agents, perhaps by ordinary secular police. So Adrian breaks off the treatment.

In the series of "doubles," the most interesting are the Rodde sisters, Clarissa and Inez—the one infatuated with a bohemian, "artistic" life on the stage, the other morbidly attracted to a bourgeois life complete with an opulent apartment, servants, expensive furniture and silver, all the heavy accouterments of a decadent, useless culture. Clarissa dies, a suicide, and Inez becomes a murderer—the instrument by which one of Adrian's "loves," albeit a minor one, is taken from him. The viciousness of Inez Rodde's egoism is all the more deadly in that it has no object beyond itself; its delight is in acting out behind the forms of an outmoded society a personal, private, sordid equation of worth with sensual passion (p. 333). Adrian, who cannot love, who is chaste out of impurity and eternally "cold," is indirectly matched with Inez, who cannot love without gluttonous, selfish desire; the two of them are trapped in a tragic egoism, despairing and doomed, the hypothetical end-products of a decadent Europe. Between them the boyish Rudi is destroyed, spurred on to a foolish proposal of marriage by Adrian's remoteness and destroyed by Inez's unnatural passion.

There are many other dialectical devices used by Mann, sometimes extravagantly and sometimes subtly. Unforgettable is the Devil as an impresario of *avant-garde* music, Saul Fitelberg, or perhaps he is a parody of the Devil himself—lively, airy, with an elegant and engaging patter that takes up page after page of chapter 37:

"*Enfin*, I cashed in on the connections I owed to the Fourberies, and they multiplied when I opened my agency for the presentation of contemporary music. Best of all, I had found myself, for as I stand here, I am a born impresario; I can't help it, it is my joy and pride, I find my satisfaction *et mes délices* in discovering talent, genius, interesting personalities, beating the drum, making society mad with enthusiasm or at least with excitement." (p. 401.)

Adrian, true to his Faustian archetype, talks of a fantastic descent to the depths of the ocean and speculates about the cosmic chill of the universe, the immeasurable and inhuman. Zeitblom, the perpetually ordinary man, is uneasy over these speculations; there is nothing in this "monstrousness" that could appeal to him as goodness, beauty, or greatness. All this is introductory to Adrian's next musical composition, "Marvels of the Universe," which parallels the "witchcraft" of Father Leverkühn. The work of music is mock-pathetic and ironic, bizarre, unpleasant, and grotesque in a solemn, formal, mathematical way (p. 274).

Now blessed with the Devil's strength, Adrian gravitates toward the unhuman, the cosmic vision before which man's puny humanism is no more significant than marsh gas. It is the vision of which Nietzsche so often speaks in his desire to break through, once and for all, the blinding human dimension of language and metaphysical pretense. In an early essay called "On Truth and Lie," Nietzsche says:

What, indeed, does man know of himself! Can he even once perceive himself completely, laid out as if in an illuminated glass case? Does not nature keep much the most from him, even about his body, to spellbind and confine him in a proud, deceptive consciousness, far from the coils of the intestines. . . . And woe to the calamitous curiosity which might peer . . . through a crack in the chamber of consciousness and look down, and sense that man rests upon the merciless, the greedy, the insatiable, the murderous, in the indifference of his ignorance—hanging in dreams, as it were, upon the back of a tiger.[11]

Hans Castorp's "dream poem of humanity," in the chapter "Snow" from *The Magic Mountain*, gives us a fanciful dramatization of Nietzsche's idea. For, having wandered into the haze, into "nothing," Hans Castorp has a vision of a lovely Edenic world in which man and nature are one—with the hideous chapel in which a child is being dismembered at its very center, the culminating point of the hallucination and of the novel itself. Castorp thinks clearly, "I have dreamed of man's state, of his courteous and enlightened social state; behind which, in the temple, the horrible blood-sacrifice was being consummated. Were they, those children of the sun, so sweetly courteous to each other, in silent recognition of that horror?" [12] For man is "the lord of counterpositions," we are told, made fruitful through his tragic dualism, and raised above the mute processes of physical nature that embody this dualism.

The dialectical tension within Adrian himself consists of his passing violently from a period of "coldness" (depression, pain, lethargy) to a period of "heat" (compulsive, maniacal activity). But, as Zeitblom notes, these periods "were not separate and without all connection, for the present state had been preparing in the former one and to some extent had already been contained in it." (p. 352.) He swings helplessly back and forth between the extremes of cold and heat, promised by the Devil as one of the punishments of hell. When Adrian finally loses his mind he comes to resemble Christ, whereas in his mature being, with his cold, aloof, mocking humor, he had resembled the Devil. Does the Devil pass over into Christ, then, absolved of his evil through his suffering, or absolved of his evil, at least, by having lost his mind? At the end of his life Adrian fulfills his own prediction for man; he is Adam who has eaten a second time from the tree of knowledge in order to fall back into innocence (p. 307). But innocence, ironically, is to be equated with the infantile.

And yet Mann suggests a "hope beyond hopelessness." In Adrian's greatest work, "The Lamentation of Dr. Faustus," there is an ending that is somehow beyond the audible ending: "one group of instruments after another retires, and what remains, as the work fades on the air, is the high G of a cello, the last word, the last fainting sound, slowly dying. . . . Then nothing more: silence, and night. But that tone which vibrates in the silence, which is no longer there, to which only the spirit harkens, and which was the voice of mourning, is no more. It changes its meaning; it abides as a light in the night." (p. 491.)

Existential Tragedy

"Who denies that a real breakthrough is worth what the tame world calls a crime? . . . There is at bottom only one problem in the world, and this is its name. How does one break through? How does one get into the open? How does one burst the cocoon and become a butterfly? [Kleist] is talking only about the aesthetic, charm, free grace, which actually is reserved to the automaton and the god; that is, to the unconscious or an endless consciousness, whereas every reflection lying between nothing and infinity kills grace. The consciousness must . . . have gone through an infinity in order that grace find itself again therein; and Adam must eat a second time from the tree of knowledge in order to fall back into the state of innocence." (p. 307–308.)

These are Adrian's words, passionate and Nietzschean, the expression of a will seeking its objectification in the world. How ironic that he should speak of every reflection between nothing and infinity as a killing of grace, dooming mankind (or the man in himself) to a purgatorial world of gracelessness, the burden of mortality torn in two directions and unable to "break through" to either pure unconsciousness or an endless consciousness! For just as Adrian aspires toward the satanic power of a god's consciousness, he is doomed by both his temperament and his physical disease to the infantile unconsciousness of a second childhood. To his icy, brittle imagination everything given is fitted for parody; earlier in the novel he has asked in bewilderment why everything seems to him its own parody. The question may very well have been Hamlet's. And, as in Hamlet's Denmark the fact of social and moral rottenness is unquestionable, so in Adrian's Europe the fact of a larger, folk-based barbarism, a true automation's unconsciousness, is a catastrophe for the precarious bourgeois order.

Dr. Faustus is a tragedy of will. But is will the seething forces of the unconscious, or is it the harnessed energy of that domain which can be controlled by the ego only at great cost, only at Faustian audacity? And what is Adrian's Devil—hallucination, or real devil, or both? The relationship between Adrian's pact with the Devil and Germany's pact with the Devil is fairly clear. Mann is always writing political allegory. The desire for a mysterious breakthrough on Adrian's part, an act that may seem a crime to the "tame world," and the breakthrough on Germany's part is fairly clear—Adrian's rise and fall precedes the rise and fall of the Third Reich. The time in which the novel is written and the time of which it is written are very important. Zeitblom confesses: "This is a quite extraordinary interweaving of time-units, destined, moreover, to include even a third: namely, the time which one day the courteous reader will take for the reading of what has been written; at which point he will be dealing with a threefold ordering of time: his own, that of the chronicler, and historic time." To which one must add a fourth dimension: the time of Mann's writing of the novel. Certainly this emphasis on time-units, this arranging of concentric circles around the fairly short life span of Adrian Leverkühn, points toward a definite historic and political framework. And, propelled backward into theological history—indeed, invited to consider what Zeitblom calls the epoch of bourgeois humanism beginning at the end of the Middle Ages—the reader understands that Adrian is to bear on his frail shoulders a tremendous symbolic burden, being at once a historical German and an ahistorical Adam, made to serve the cause of political allegory as well as the larger cause of mythical allegory.

Critics who interpret *Dr. Faustus* as a devastating critique of an imperialist epoch surely miss the point; one thinks of the extraordinary claims of the Marxist critic, Lukács, who applauds Adrian at one point for discovering "the way which leads to Marx," [13] but writes him off as a victim of the disintegrating values of his society. Certainly the political symbolism of the novel is highly significant: is not little Helmut Institoris, instructor in art and aesthetics and Inez's cuckolded husband, a terrible parody of the age and of Adrian as well? He who celebrates the Italian Renaissance as a time that "reeked of blood and beauty," and who himself must lead a life of scrupulous regularity, is a mockery of Adrian's impulse toward the twice-barbaric that will break through to the future. And the various members of the Munich circle (nearly all of them physically diseased or somehow incapacitated for active life) express comically grotesque enthusiasms for the coming era, applauding violence and waste and the elimination of the unfit—though they themselves are obviously unfit. The most despicable character in the novel is the Jewish scholar, Dr. Breisacher, whose cultural barbarism and argumentative love of paradox prefigures the glorification of the irrational that will result in wholesale slaughter of the Jews—and, if the reeking of blood and beauty is desired, if a breakthrough is desired, why not a wholesale slaughter of the Jews?

Mann is fascinated by the morbid passivity and suicidal masochism of the German intellectual community. When insanity becomes history, it seems to become sane again; no standards remain. The line between aestheticism and barbarism is uncertain. These intellectuals give themselves over to the new era before it is even upon them, prophesizing the violence of the future all too accurately. But to say, as Lukács says, that Adrian's tragedy lies in his attitude toward social and historical reality[14] is to suggest that the problem of the artist is not psychological at all, but simply social. A rearrangement of society will eradicate the artist's sufferings and make his art miraculously *per du* with humanity—a transformation that is very nearly mystical. It is simply not true that the artist's problem in the modern age is tied up with modern bourgeois individualism, which is in its turn a result of imperialism; on the contrary, the very nature of the artist predetermines his isolation, and it is the isolation of the artist that makes possible his art, his art that justifies his tragic isolation. Nor is it true that the artist searches for truth of any social or moral nature.

"Relationship is everything," Adrian has told Zeitblom. It is ambiguity. To the existential imagination things do not exist except through relationships; they do not, strictly speaking, exist in themselves. As Nietzsche says in *Human, All-Too-Human*:

Apparently, [the artist] fights for the higher dignity and significance of man; in truth, he does not want to give up the most effective presuppositions of his art: the fantastic, mythical, uncertain, extreme, the sense for the symbolic, the overestimation of the person, the faith in some miraculous element in the genius. Thus he considers the continued existence of his kind of creation more important than scientific devotion to the truth in every form, however plain.[15]

By definition, the artist is asocial—not necessarily antisocial, but asocial. He has no clear relationship with society. Delivered over to an ideology, caught up in a historical certainty, he fails to be faithful to the ambiguous—hence, the feverish and unconvincing redemptions in Dostoevski, which seem to follow so violently from the convincing nightmares that are his true interest. Erich Kahler interprets Adrian's predicament as the tragic inability to relate, to achieve redemption through relationship with life: "the Faustian drama is revealed as the dialectical predicament of every creature, the inborn paradox of life." [16] And this is surely Mann's point, at least in part: the paradox of life is inborn and not socially determined. But to settle for an interpretation that aligns Adrian with all of mankind—Adrian as simply Adam, desirous of eating once again of the tabooed fruit—is to ignore the worth of Adrian's compositions. And surely Mann has not gone to such extraordinary lengths in analyzing and admiring these nonexistent musical works for no purpose.

Adrian is Mann's most exalted embodiment of the artist. Unlike Aschenbach, who is another European genius though a "classical" writer, Adrian makes a conscious choice of nightmares: he arranges and wills his disaster. The strange passivity with which he sends Rudi to his own beloved to propose for him is not really strange at all. He does not want to love her, he wants instead to lose her, and so it happens that he loses her; it is a choice, perhaps half-conscious, but a choice nevertheless. When, near the end of his career, he comes to love his nephew and is torn apart by the child's terrible suffering and death, it is clear that he laments his fate, but not clear that he would have traded it for another. Adrian becomes Faust; he walks in the footsteps of Faust, in the fulfillment of a destiny that was willed and from which he does not draw back in terror or self-pity. Though Mann has said in a letter that Adrian represents only a single type of artist,[17] this does not exclude the possibility of Adrian's being the highest type of artist, nor does it really exclude the possibility of Mann's remark being quite irrelevant to his own work. If Adrian's life is seen as wasted, then there is no tragedy; but if his musical compositions are truly great, if he is truly a genius who could have fulfilled his genius by no other means than this "pact with the Devil," then his story is a tragedy. It seems obvious from the novel that Mann apotheosizes Adrian as composer (music being the highest art) and makes clear the paradox that his work balances his sufferings, and perhaps even the sufferings of those around him. Existential tragedy may be differentiated from classical tragedy in that no "mistake" occurs; there is not a point at which the tragic hero could have taken another direction. Having chosen another direction, he would not have become himself—which, in Nietzchean terms, is the only imperative—and having chosen this particular direction, this particular destiny, he comes to a "tragic" end as a human being but achieves a triumph denied to human beings generally.

Does art in *Dr. Faustus* "tragically lament the loss of its own mystery"? [18] Or is this a question from Zeitblom's point of view? Art as expression of conscious will—the highest expression of will—discloses not simply the alternatives of the endless unconscious or the endless conscious, but justifies the intermediary realm that Adrian calls graceless. Suffering is justified by its art, and, curiously enough, art is justified by its suffering: "the value of a thing sometimes does not lie in that which one attains by it, but in what one pays for it—what it costs us," as Nietzsche says in *The Twilight of the Idols*. There is the slightly repulsive suggestion in both Nietzsche and Mann that the artist expends himself in his art and, having accomplished it, is finished as a human being.

Two central questions: what is will? what is Adrian's Devil—fantasy, or reality, or both? Let the Devil exist as a given, not simply as Adrian's eloquent repressed consciousness (in the manner of Dostoevski), for otherwise what are we to do with the comic diabolicalism of Saul Fitelberg and of Professor Schleppfuss, "your humble servant"? It is fashionable to insist upon the psychological basis of literary devils, who are an embarrassment to a naturalistic epoch. Therefore, it is no surprise to note that the dust jacket of a popular edition of *Dr. Faustus* shows us Adrian and his tempter facing each other with precisely the same expression and the same face—in short, they are the same person; this is acceptable enough for most readers; indeed, it is the only acceptable devil.

But Mann is not a writer of naturalism. He deals with historical reality, and his bizarre stories take place in real countries and real cities, but he has no commitment to the limitations of naturalism; the "fantastic, mythical, uncertain, extreme, the sense for the symbolic . . . the faith in some miraculous element"—all this is Mann, thoroughly Mann. In *The Magic Mountain* there is a chapter ambiguously titled "Highly Questionable," in which Hans Castorp's dead cousin, Joachim, appears at a seance. He is wearing a strange uniform, and, as Hermann J. Weigand points out in his study of the novel, one must know that "no civilian of prewar days could possibly have brought forth out of his subconsciousness a vision of a soldier in garb like this." [19] Therefore, the novel's walls fall back. This fantastic image is not Hans Castorp's projection, but a true prophecy of the future, and so the novel itself breaks through the boundaries of a conventional naturalism. Mann's Devil may be in Adrian's head or outside it.

As Mann says through the Devil, this tendency to insist upon the objective is petty bourgeois: "As you see me, so I exist to you. What serves it to ask whether I really am? Is not 'really' what works, is not truth experience and feeling?" (p. 242.) The accidents of Dr. Erasmi and Dr. Zimbalist are factually true in the narrative of *Dr. Faustus*, just as certain irrefutable clues in Henry James's *The Turn of the Screw* point toward the existence of the ghosts, disappointing as this may be to argumentative critics. Indeed, the matched improbabilities of Mann and James suggest nothing more than the various improbabilities of any work of art, usually tacitly accepted because they are behind the scenes.

As a drama of will-made-conscious, *Dr. Faustus* is terrifying because it is hermetic, and that which is hermetic excludes all accident, all chance. This is Mann's point precisely. "When I hear of hearing!" Adrian exclaims. "In my view it is quite enough if something has been heard *once*; I mean when the artist thought it out." So, for the composer the actual written composition is far removed from its original vital reality; it has become material, it exists for others, it has been bypassed. There is no wonder in the fact that Adrian avoids attending presentations of his own work, for his having thought it out, his exercise of original will, precludes any further interest of his in it. Just as the artist's will creates his art in a godly manner, in pure thought, so does the artist's will create itself. As psychology this is bewildering, for it is Sartre's psychology, the theory of "endless consciousness"—one creates one's essence, one makes himself, man has no nature but only a history—far from the modest speculations of Freud, far into the realm of the mystic and the terrifying, in short, Mann as Schopenhauer.

For behind Nietzsche stands Schopenhauer, the "father of all modern psychology" in Mann's opinion, because he is the first psychologist of the will. *The World as Will and Idea* is an extraordinary accomplishment, says Mann, a work whose meaning is expressed totally in its title and is present in every line.[20] The bipolar nature of man is analyzed by Schopenhauer without sentiment and found to consist of a terrible opposition: the will and the idea, the blind primitive force of will, or life, and the enlightened, would-be autonomous force of the intellect. The struggle is dramatic and endless, though will has its ultimate victory in the reproductive life of the species; man splits in two, drawn by the erotic in one direction and by the principles of the mind in another, unable to synthesize the two. Mann is impatient with fashionable twentieth-century trends of reacting against classical rationalism in favor of the unconscious, the deliberate glorification of instinct. In Schopenhauer's essay, "Transcendent Speculations on Apparent Design in the Fate of the Individual," the extraordinary theory is developed that life, like dreams, is directed by man's will, and that the accidental is only accidental in appearance. "It is our own will," Mann says, "that unconsciously appears as inexorable objective destiny." [21]

So it is possible for Mann to believe in and to create more-than-human men like Adrian, whose asceticism (a conscious fight against the blinding instinctive will) leads them to a higher consciousness, a refinement of the will to the point at which the will creates itself. Thus Adrian creates himself and his destiny; his fall has depended upon the "disposition, the readiness, the invitation" (p. 233), and it depends also upon his decision, which is a decision for disease. That which is diseased and that which is criminal blend, in Mann as in Nietzsche, the criminal being a type of strength under unfavorable circumstances: "a strong human being made sick." [22] Nietzsche sees society (Christian society) as tame and emasculating, in which a natural human being necessarily degenerates into a criminal. Zeitblom speculates that the process of sublimation is faulty in such a person as Adrian: "the proudest intellectuality stands in the most immediate relation of all the animal, to naked instinct, is given over most shamefully to it . . ." (p. 147). This supports Adrian's conviction that intellectual interest, not love, is the strongest human emotion, for love is not possible in a being in whom sublimation does not work. And Zeitblom counters shrewdly with a definition of Adrian's "interest"; it is a kind of love "from which the animal warmth has withdrawn" (p. 69).

For the higher human being, then, there is the possibility of utter freedom—of breaking through outmoded forms. The ego is unified with the world; when one perceives that the apparently objective and accidental is a result of the soul's creation, one understands the tragic confinement of this freedom. The existential figure creates himself through his actions; he cannot make mistakes, because that is a contradiction in terms. Adrian does not make any mistake. His ego expands to include a participation in other selves, as Mann believes certain human beings transcend their historical reality through this abrogation of the individual in the "type." Adrian's role as Leverkühn is individual enough and entirely believable, but his role as Faust is one he grows into, one which his suffering (over the loss of his beloved, of Rudi, and most of all, of his nephew) educates him into knowing. Mann was fascinated by the confidence-game of the early Fausts—Simon of one century and Helmstätter of another—not simply because of their audacity and success, but because of their apparent ability to transform themselves, to abrogate their self-ness in the type. Hence, in 1526, Mann speculates, Helmstätter was not merely the successor of Faustus; in a sense he became Faustus. It was an age of "great sympathetic understanding of the myth." [23] In the famous 1936 essay, "Freud and the Future," Mann discusses this mythologizing of the self in relationship to *Joseph and His Brothers*; it is the movement from bourgeois individualism to the mythical and typical, the timeless creation, that characterizes this work, a religious gesture, a celebration, a making present of the past. So with Adrian. Unlike "Adrian Leverkühn," he invites a large and varied audience to hear "The Lamentation of Dr. Faustus"; he has become Faust, who likewise invited an audience to whom he confessed his sins.

The paradox in Mann lies in his commitment to and his strenuous approval of the dialectical process as a technical means, and his ultimate mystical belief in the unity of the ego and the world. *Dr. Faustus*, like *The Magic Mountain*, concerns itself with form and formlessness, the discipline of living and the temptation of dying, attempting in its very pages a synthesis of the two that cannot come about except through art, that is, through artifice. The struggle between the will and the ego, or the id and the ego, is pathetic and comic and tragic simultaneously; but, viewed as idea alone, viewed as the total creation of man's will represented through art, it makes a "significant spectacle" and transcends mortality to become timeless and immortal, as the inhuman will itself is immortal. For life in the myth, Mann says, is a liberation from the individual and the doomed, and "it becomes a feast." [24]

Where to Mann the technique of imitation by mythologizing is an expansive, liberating event, to most writers of the mid-twentieth century it is a technique of brutalizing diminishment. In his discussion of Samuel Beckett, George Steiner remarks that Beckett's anti-drama is an attempt to "bar from the stage all forms of mobility and natural communication," the result being crippled and monotonous. Drama—and we may extend this to mean literature itself—cannot endure without "the creation of characters endowed with the miracle of independent life." [25] In Mann the creation of characters is playfully questionable, but so bizarre and sly is Mann's genius that one cannot ever quite know whether the ambiguity is to be resolved on the naturalistic or the fantastical side.

For our brilliant contemporary, Eugene Ionesco, there is no ambiguity in life. Life is a dream, or, rather, a series of dreams—interrupted, betrayed, brutally shaped, shapeless. He has transmuted the "real" totally into the fantastic. There is no question of the existence of independent life, the creation of "true characters," the freedom from an overwhelming and claustrophobic joke. Everything is problematic, symbolic, but only crudely "psychological" (no normal psyches are involved), whimsical and abrupt in transition, dominated by an idea or an anti-idea. Most of the background is left unexpressed, like the background of a hasty dream, and the foreground is likely to be cluttered with colorful but distracting details scrupulously recounted. The intense complications of life in Mann have given way, in Ionesco, to an irreducible "reality"—the vivid, cartoonlike shapes of humanity endlessly rehearsing humanity's ancient tragic rites.

9

IONESCO'S
Dances of Death

There is no solution to the intolerable, and only that which is intolerable is truly theatrical.[1]

Most literature deals consciously or unconsciously with the problem of reality: it asks what is real in the world, which values are real, which without foundation and therefore false or evil. One can often see on stage the manipulation of plot to bring about the unmasking of appearances, since drama is a spectacle severely limited by time and place, though it is not always certain what has been exorcized and what acclaimed as real. Clearly, such traditional comedies as *Tartuffe* and *The Silent Woman* point out their "morals" without ambiguity; tragedies like *Antigone* or *Macbeth*, fortified by poetry of direct and sometimes sententious statement, do not

225

suffer from ambiguity. But what is one to say of *Troilus and Cressida*, of *Antony and Cleopatra*, to a lesser degree of *Volpone*? If the process of unmasking is the young Troilus' education, how can it be an affirmative matter if it points toward nihilism? If Antony is not to be denied his illusions but remains, even at death, as firmly himself as ever, in what sense can the tragic experience have occurred? And in *Volpone* one is torn between reacting simply, by rejoicing at the proper unmasking of knaves, and reacting in quite another way, as if the spectacle of comic knaves has become a spectacle of men who are knaves and who have demonstrated their own admirable skill in perceiving what is real in the midst of what is hypocritical: a skill that invites the spectator to applaud it, despite the shabby ends to which it is put. Here the dichotomy between appearance and reality is blurred; one feels the playwright deliberately withhold or qualify his meaning.

Eugene Ionesco's dramatic works deal with the tension between appearances and realities, and it is not simply the so-called "absurd" tradition of his plays that perplexes and sometimes irritates, but the failure—the deliberate failure—of Ionesco to substitute for cheap and devastated appearances a reality that is permanent. His "tragic farces," "anti-plays," "comic dramas," "naturalistic comedies," and "pseudo-dramas" have in common a process of disintegration that is, in a way, the precise opposite of the traditional process of revelation that structurally determines the pattern of tragedy or comedy. As the professor of *The Lesson* explains:

One must be able to subtract too. It's not enough to integrate, you must also disintegrate. That's the way life is. That's philosophy. That's science. That's progress, civilization.

What is shocking about Ionesco's world is that the clearing away of deceptive appearances does not result in a celebration of reality (in a sense even Troilus' bitter discovery is a "celebration" of the power of truth), but results simply in nothing. When appearances are demolished, nothing remains. There is no underlying "reality": reality is no more than the sum of petty trifles, the clocked universe of *The Bald Soprano* that parodies our worlds of endless details that few men can transcend. Ionesco's art is the tragic expression of those who cannot transcend the crippling biological, social, and accidental banality of their lives. The only "transcending" is death, but this is surely a parody of what man has always meant by the transcending of his mortal life. As Jack complains in *Jack, or the Submission:*

And how to escape? They've boarded up the doors, the windows with nothing, they've taken away the stairs. . . . One can't get out through the attic anymore, there's no way out up there. . . . If one can't exit through the attic, there's always the cellar, yes, the cellar. It would be better to go out down there than to be here. Anything is preferable to my present situation.

Perhaps two of Ionesco's plays seem to be affirmative: *Rhinoceros,* usually interpreted as the story of one man's refusal to degenerate into the beast, and *Amédée, or How to Get Rid of It,* in which an apparent intellectual, a playwright, finally frees himself of his imprisonment in a loveless marriage by transcending—literally—his environment and disappearing from the stage. Both these plays, however, are affirmative in gesture rather than tone. *Rhinoceros,* to be discussed below, can be seen as more skeptical than it usually is, and is in any case dominated by an atmosphere of impending doom as one witnesses all

227

of mankind gladly changing into beasts; *Amédée*, with its fantastic ending, in a sense implies that the only way one can break out of a corpse-haunted and mushroom-infested existence is by violating nature—an act inaccessible in the "real" world. Yet even in these plays Ionesco is working with a structural process of disintegration, despite his development so far as traditional form is concerned (beginnings, middles, ends).

Ionesco's first play, *The Bald Soprano* (1950), inspired by his experiences while trying to learn English out of a conversation handbook, is an "anti-play" that reaches beyond its most immediate satiric objects (the relentless banality of conversation; the middle-class English; the expository and other awkwardnesses of the stage) to suggest a comic-bitter tragedy of human relationships. Ionesco saw it as demonstrating the "tragedy of language" [2] and, as in several of his other important plays, it is language that is seen as the most human of human accomplishments, the most potentially majestic and therefore, in its failure, the most ignoble. Usually one comes to a play to witness actors impersonating characters related, somehow, in a work of art, but here one sees actors impersonating actors impersonating "characters." The visual stage offers an ideal medium for the peculiar effect Ionesco wants: the reader of *The Bald Soprano* can skim through the nonsense conversations and be amused, but the spectator is forced to experience the play as well as to understand it, to feel the anguish and viciousness of frustrated communication welling up in himself as it wells up and ultimately overcomes the Smiths and the Martins, respectable and entirely recognizable folk. Also, the spectator can measure the language against the tone and action. The scene between the Martins in which they discover through a series of questions and answers that they reside in the same room, sleep in the same bed, have the same child, and that they are therefore man and wife, is to be played "against the text": that is, while the couple arrive at what should be a devastating truth, they express their wonderment in "drawling, monotonous, singsong" voices. One needs to witness, also, the rendering of the bizarre into the banal, especially typified by the clock that strikes a surprising number of times but is interpreted by the Smiths as behaving normally. (When the clock strikes seventeen, Mrs. Smith declares it is nine o'clock.) Later, we see the banal transformed into the bizarre, as Mrs. Martin talks about a man, properly dressed, tying his shoelace; and Mr. Martin tops this by telling of another man reading a newspaper. "What a character!" say the Smiths. "Perhaps it was the same man!" There is no observer, unless perhaps it is the fire chief, whose vision of life is dependable, for though he fits in very well with the demented world of the Smiths and the Martins, he is able to assess himself in relationship to it: "I admit . . . all this is very subjective . . . but this is my conception of the world. My world. My dream. My ideal. . . ." Ionesco himself is quoted in Richard N. Coe's book, *Eugene Ionesco*,[3] in a remark that seems to extend the fire chief's:

. . . nothing is capable of seeming to me . . . any more improbable than anything else, for everything is brought down to the same level, everything is drowned in the general improbability and unlikelihood of the universe itself. The fact of existence, the very use of language—these are what seem to me inconceivable. . . . It is existence itself that seems unimaginable; and, that being so, there is nothing *within* existence that has the power to startle my credulity. (p. 29.)

229

The scene in *The Bald Soprano* in which a doorbell rings mysteriously though no one is at the door, leading Mrs. Smith to conclude that it is categorically true that when one hears the doorbell it is because there is never anyone there, is similar to the "discovery" scene between the Martins in its parodying of conventional reasoning, whether "empirical" or "logical." Experience teaches us nothing, logic teaches us nothing. Attempts at rational deductive logic are thwarted, and with them man's attempts at sanity, so that one is destined, finally, to degenerate into the beast. Ionesco's rejection of logic is expressed in *Rhinoceros* also. Here a logician (who later turns into a rhinoceros) explains the syllogism to an impressed listener:

L. : The cat has four paws. Isidore and Fricot both have four paws. Therefore Isidore and Fricot are cats.
G. : My dog has four paws.
L. : Then it's a cat.
G. : . . . Logic is a very beautiful thing.

The lesson continues:

L. : All cats die. Socrates is dead. Therefore Socrates is a cat.
G. : And he's got four paws. That's true. I've got a cat named Socrates.

But while such absurd "reasoning" will never discover the truth in *Rhinoceros*, "experience" fails just as completely. Ionesco is relentless in his antiromantic rejection of the primacy of experience, which seeks to fill in gaps of knowledge by the subjective delusions of particular individuals. If "nothing" is the truth that is to be learned, then it is necessary to reject all systems that teach truth as something real, something available through investigation or logic. Richard N. Coe in his study of Ionesco discusses the influence on him of the "Collège de Pataphysique," a movement or climate of mind that rejects what we would call common sense and the laws of contradiction. Theoretically, Pataphysics cannot be explained in nonpataphysical terms, but it appears to have its basis in an insistence upon the futility of scientific law. It denies a deterministic universe and, simultaneously, the whole structure of causality upon which our civilization practically and philosophically is constructed. Each event in the world is unique in itself; it has not been "caused," is not related to a causal structure that has determined and therefore "explained" it. Since it is singular, it will not recur. Pataphysics sees only the particular, never the general (which does not exist), and in this way reminds us of the vague, common tenet of existentialism, that what is real is only what is experienced, as Kierkegaard would say dogmatically, by an existing individual at a particular time and place; this experience cannot be abstracted from the circumstances of its occurrence. Each event and each individual are then exceptions in history. If this sounds nihilistic, it should be remembered that the Pataphysical movement is a protest against a predetermined and therefore soulless scientific world, a parallel with the twentieth-century movement back toward tradition, whether Neo-Thomism or the intellectual asceticism of a T. E. Hulme or a T. S. Eliot. Pataphysics is a reaction against something, and the most pataphysical of Ionesco's plays, *The Bald Soprano*, is at once a brilliantly original work and a dead end.

Ionesco's admirers claim that this play announces the ruin. The progression from cliché to cliché that is climaxed by a rapid-fire barrage of *non sequiturs* ("One walks on his feet, but one heats with electricity or coal";

"He who sells an ox today will have an egg tomorrow")
and then by a dizzying rush into pure noise is a tour de
force that cannot be repeated. As soon as the fire chief,
himself a parody of a hero-savior figure from the outside
world who should come and put things right, leaves the
Smiths' home, their disintegration is rapid. The evening
ends in complete ferocity as the characters scream words
and sounds at one another, unable to know why they are
suddenly so excited. Language has disintegrated so that
its symbolic or human level is lost completely; words are
simply noises that have no abstract referents. Yet these
truly nonsensical words (caca, Krishnamurti), screamed
out with passion, come to have more emotional significance than the exchange of meaningless social drivel that
has preceded them. Because they cannot communicate,
the Smiths and the Martins must descend from the
bourgeois human level that has constituted their identity; they become beasts. The "fire" of irrationality overcomes them, as the same fire overcomes the professor in
The Lesson and Jack in *Jack*. The maid's poem, "The
Fire," anticipates the relentless lyric progression of this
overwhelming irrational force:

> The polypoids (*sic*) were burning in the wood
>> A stone caught fire
>> The castle caught fire
>> The forest caught fire
>> The men caught fire
>> The women caught fire
>> The birds caught fire
>> The fish caught fire
>> The water caught fire
>> The sky caught fire
>> The ashes caught fire

The smoke caught fire
The fire caught fire
Everything caught fire
Caught fire, caught fire.

Ionesco mentioned in an essay in the *Tulane Drama Review* for Spring, 1960, that "The Smiths, the Martins, can no longer talk because they can no longer think; they can no longer think *because they can no longer feel passions.* They can no longer be; they can become anybody, anything, for, having lost their identity, they assume the identity of others . . . they are interchangeable." The cyclical ending of the play simply emphasizes the comic futility that underlies the "tragedy of language": there can be no moment of truth, hence no conclusion to the play. It is the fate of the Smiths and the Martins, and by extension everyone, to re-enact endlessly this devastation of appearances climaxed by a loss of human dignity, bringing with it no romantic intuitive knowledge of life.

The Lesson (1950), though more conventional theater, in outline almost an anecdote, is constructed along the same lines as *The Bald Soprano:* the disintegration of human sanity or order, symbolized by language. The professor, a stereotyped caricature of a pedant—he wears a little white beard, pince-nez, a black skullcap, a long black schoolmaster's coat, trousers and shoes of black, white collar, a black tie—and his student, a lively good-natured girl of eighteen, are involved in a "lesson" that continues the degradation of humanity begun in the first play. Where the Smiths and the Martins do no more than scream at one another, the professor translates his frustration into action and kills his pupil. The girl represents life, health, rather simple-minded normality; she can only add, does not know how to subtract. The pro-

233

fessor represents, at first, an extreme of intellectual development that seems to have passed over entirely from the human. "We can't be sure of anything, young lady, in this world," he says politely at the start of the lesson; in each play a character says something very much like this, understatement to be sure, but representing a moment of usually uncharacteristic insight.

The professor's discourse on language is a brilliant piece of private, pedantic madness: words mean the same thing in any language, Spanish, Latin, Italian, French, Portuguese, Romanian, Sardinian, or Sardanapalian, and that which distinguishes one language from another is "an intangible thing, something intangible that one is able to perceive only after very long study. . . . One must have a feeling for it." We soon see that "truth" is the possession of the professor alone; the girl, under his power, languishes and finally dies because of his authority to control and interpret the truth. Language becomes a means of dictatorial power and ultimately the means of death itself. The "tragedy of language" is here italicized by the obvious sadistic relish the professor feels as he attacks the girl, his fortieth victim, suggesting the sadistic-masochistic relationship inherent between professor and pupil, ruler and ruled, possessor of truth and the ignorant masses. In *The Killer* the fascistic Mother Peep and her Geese continue the Professor's manipulation of language in an episode that ends with the death of someone who has opposed her:

PEEP

When tyranny is restored we'll call it discipline and liberty. The misfortune of one is the happiness of all. . . . Our reason will be founded on anger. And there'll be soup kitchens for all.

234

CROWD

Long live Mother Peep! . . . .

PEEP

Objectivity is subjective in the para-scientific age.

And she continues:

They'll be stupid, that means intelligent. Cowardly, that means brave. Clear-sighted, that means blind. . . . We'll march backwards and be in the forefront of history. . . . If an ideology doesn't apply to real life, we'll say it does and it'll all be perfect. . . . We'll replace the myths . . . by slogans . . . and the latest platitudes!

A drunkard argues with her and Mother Peep, hitting him with a briefcase, says, "Let's have a free discussion!" After a fight involving Mother Peep and her geese, the drunkard is apparently dead; Mother Peep says, "My geese have liquidated him. But only physically." So powerful is language in Ionesco's imagination that the word "knife" can be used to slay the Professor's pupil. He then puts on a swastika armband and is reassured by the maid that the townspeople will not bother him since they are accustomed to his behavior. The play ends with the doorbell ringing and another pupil arriving for the lesson.

Ionesco is obviously fascinated and obsessed by the power that resides in language and therefore in those who have the power to control the meanings of words. Against nearly any other obstacle man can protect himself; but the confusion of language annihilates man's reason completely, for it is only through language that one is to be distinguished from the beasts. Ionesco's hatred of Nazism has clearly influenced most of his work. He speaks of Nazism as being "Nature against mind": irrationality against rationality, "instinct" against intellect;

yet it is ironic that he can suggest nowhere in his plays that "mind" is capable of making life endurable. The Smiths and the Martins suffer at first from sheer inertia, a lack of passion; at the end they are overcome by emotion; but nowhere are they real human beings. The Professor's "mind" is victim to his own "nature," so that the accomplishments of the intellect are in themselves always suspect, controlled as they are by the unconscious. Ionesco has said grimly that he has "no other images of the world except those of evanescence and brutality, vanity and rage, nothingness or hideous, useless hatred. [4] What is extraordinary is his ability to translate this pessimism into an art so beautifully managed, so cleanly and tragically comic.

Jack, or the Submission (1950) is another story of disintegration, here of a pseudo-tragic or art hero's capitulation to conformity. Significantly, the setting calls for a picture on a wall "that doesn't represent anything." This is the reality the play moves toward: the annihilation of the identity of the hero rather than an affirmation of it. Jack conforms initially by succumbing to his parents' protestations and saying that he loves "hashed brown potatoes"; he conforms finally by saying, "I'll marry you" to a girl of exceptional physical disabilities. She wins him by evoking in him an irresistible sexual desire, thereby trapping him, as she tells him the story of a flaming horse. Jack joins in the story in spite of himself:

JACK

His mane is blazing! His beautiful mane . . . He cries, he whinnies. Han! han! The flame flashes up. . . .

ROBERTA II

The more he gallops, the more the flame spreads. He is

mad, he's terrified, he's in pain, he's sick, he's afraid, he's in pain . . . it flames up, it spreads all over his body!

Jack becomes exhausted when the story is over and says he is thirsty. Roberta says:

Come on . . . don't be afraid . . . I'm moist. . . . My necklace is made of mud, my breasts are dissolving, my pelvis is wet, I've got water in my crevasses, I'm sinking down. . . . In my belly, there are pools, swamps . . . I've got a house of clay. I'm always cool. . . . There's moss . . . big flies, cockroaches, sowbugs, toads. Under the wet covers they make love . . . they're swollen with happiness! . . . My mouth trickles down, my legs trickle, my naked shoulders trickle, my hair trickles, everything trickles down, runs, everything trickles, the sky trickles down, the stars run, trickle down, trickle. . . .

Jack cannot resist. His submission to the biological imprisonment Roberta represents is applauded by the families, who come in and surround the squatting, embracing couple. They circle around in a ridiculous dance, a parody of the community celebration of marriage in romantic comedy, in itself a faint adumbration of ceremonies of fertility; but here it is only the physical level that is acknowledged. Ionesco says of the dance, in what must surely be an exceptional stage direction, "All this must produce in the audience a feeling of embarrassment, awkwardness, and shame." The characters squat, miaowing, moaning, and croaking; they have lost their identity as human beings. The love story of Jack and Roberta is continued in *The Future is in Eggs*, where Roberta hatches countless basketsful of eggs to the families' cries of "Production! Production! Long live production! Long live the white race!" The eggs are to hatch into cannon fodder, omelettes, athletes, officers, diplomats, bankers, popes, policemen, nationalists, radicals, Marxists, drunkards, Catholics, stairs, and Israelites of the future: a stunning image of the proliferation of humanity without souls.

This great anonymous world is invited to hear the Old Man's message in *The Chairs* (1951), but when the desks arrive they are visible only to the Old Man and his wife: are they therefore private hallucination, or is the "reality" the vision that the world is nothing and it is only by the magical process of the theater that we as spectators are granted this realization? Here we witness an Old Man and an Old Woman, aged ninety-five and ninety-four, prepare for the presentation of the man's message to the world, to be delivered to a gigantic gathering of people (janitors, chemists, violinists, proletarians, alienists, alienated, and so on) by a professional Orator. The insularity of pure self suggested by their environment (they live on a tower on an island; the stage is bathed in green light) is heightened by the several motifs that bind the play together: the man's lament that the light is retreating, that once it was daylight at midnight but now, at six o'clock, it is already dark; the typical pathetic musings of the wife (if he had only had a little ambition in life he could have been head president, head king, head doctor); the old man's genuine faith that he has a message to deliver to humanity. The guests arrive and the old couple fill up the stage with chairs in which they presumably sit, carrying on conversations with them, flattering them, being tempted by them to surrender to youthful delusions of romantic love. The metaphorical dimensions of Ionesco's art are nowhere more powerful than in *The Chairs*, which creates out of nothing a semblance of a world, and evokes through the desultory ramblings of the old couple's conversation fragments of wasted, confused, and quite ordinary lives. Thus the mother speaks wistfully of their only son, who left them at the age of seven, accusing them of killing birds. The child cries bitterly:

> . . . you kill all the birds, all the birds. . . . You're lying, you've betrayed me! The streets are full of dead birds, of dying baby birds. . . . The sky is red with blood. . . . You've betrayed me, I adored you, I believed you to be good . . . the streets are full of dead birds, you've torn out their eyes. . . . It's you who are responsible.

The Old Woman asks, "What does that mean, 'responsible'?" Here, in surrealistic, hyperbolic terms, the adult and child worlds clash and part, the adult's confusion over the "responsibility" for evil in the world symptomatic of the helpless ignorance of maturity—for to the old woman the birds are not dying, but singing; this is her truth—and not of its conscious evil, for the calculated deliberation of responsibility is perhaps beyond the grasp of such ordinary folk. This is the pathos of life: as much the turning of the child's sharp-focused view into the adult's blindness as the stark terror of the child's discovery of brutality in the world. At the same time, the Old Man recounts his abandonment of his mother, who died lying in a ditch with a lily of the valley in her hand, while he went to a dance. He says, "I know, I know, sons always abandon their mothers, and they more or less kill their fathers. . . . Life is like that . . . but I, I suffer from it . . . and the others, they don't. . . ." Just as the usually respected role of aged seer is here parodied, so are

239

these expressions of fundamental human truths, twisted out of their pathetic connotations and rendered comic.

Activity is heightened onstage; more and more "guests" arrive, so that the old couple are running back and forth feverishly with chairs. The woman sells programs, Eskimo pies, fruit drops, until she is hemmed in by the crowd and is unable to move. Then there are fanfares in the wings: the main door opens with a great crash: a very powerful, cold, empty light shines through. The Emperor himself arrives. The old couple are at the very height of their happiness, for the Emperor is their Savior, is God, who reduces them to barking dogs and slavish courtiers. When the Orator arrives—he is a "real" person, though dressed pretentiously and haughtily indifferent to the Old Man—the Old Man says, "Our existence can come to an end in this apotheosis. . . . If I have been long unrecognized, underestimated by my contemporaries, it is because it had to be. . . . What matters all that now when I am leaving to you, my dear Orator and friend . . . the responsibility of radiating upon posterity the light of my mind." After throwing confetti and paper streamers on the Emperor and the Orator, the Old Man and his wife commit suicide by jumping out of windows into the ocean. The Orator seems not to notice. Then the Orator decides to begin: but he turns out to be deaf and dumb, and the message he communicates to the audience is unintelligible. Is this the Old Man's message, or has the Orator betrayed the Old Man? The ending remains ambiguous. After the Orator walks out petulantly, we hear for the first time the human noises of the invisible crowd: laughter, murmurs, shhh's, coughs. The confusion of the real audience, the real world represented by those "really" attending the play, is shared by that of the invisible audience. No hallucination after all, the invisible people demonstrate themselves present in the way that the world must always be present for the poet or prophet or playwright: they are both real and unreal, "there" and not there at all. One sees Ionesco the playwright expressing his comic anguish at his own role, trying to communicate to a faceless audience a message that is at the same time meaningful and grotesquely absurd. The "audience" is as mysterious as the message, finally, and the isolation of the self that seeks to transcend the masses can never be overcome by any gesture, however tragic or comic or both. What in another era might be seen as tragic is taken in our century as tragically comic. *The Chairs* is a play really created about nothing, a brilliant magical contriving of something out of nothing that passes, finally, into nothing at the end.

Yet one feels that its effectiveness as art belies the theme of absurdity, for if the absurd is, as Ionesco says, that which has no purpose, or goal, or objective, then the creation of a coherent piece of art is a gesture of anti-absurdity. So, with the apparently hopeless world of Samuel Beckett's novels, *The Unnamable* and *Malone Dies* in particular, in which the desire to establish artistic order rises mysteriously out of the chaos of life:

"But what matter whether I was born or not, have lived or not, am dead or merely dying, I shall go on doing as I have always done, not knowing what it is I do, nor who I am, nor where I am, nor if I am. Yes, a little creature, I shall try to make a little creature, to hold in my arms, a little creature in my image. . . ." [5]

241

And, later in the novel, Malone says that he "must state the facts, without trying to understand, to the end." [6] Why must one state the facts? The gesture of message-making becomes more significant, finally, than the substance of the message itself. The Old Man of *The Chairs* is heroic at the same time that he is foolish, not simply because he never sees himself unmasked but because his attempt at a message, futile as it is, is nevertheless one of the few positive gestures one can find in Ionesco.

The Killer (1957) and *Rhinoceros* (1959), full-length plays, are constructed about single poetic images, like the first four plays, but are more coherently developed and present characters who behave in psychologically conventional ways—up to a point. Both build to powerful climaxes, but the minute-by-minute texture of their dialogue is not as compelling or as wildly hilarious as that of the earlier, more experimental plays. *The Killer* deals with the irreparable fallen nature of man and the ubiquitous presence of death by imagining a beautiful radiant city, a city of light, created by architectural geniuses yet ruined by the presence of an unknown, insane killer. That the radiant city is a poetic image for the inner life of man, his spiritual strivings against a material chaos, is evident from the musings of the "hero," Bérenger:

I do so need another life, a new life. Different surroundings, a different setting . . . a background that would answer some profound need inside, which would be somehow . . . the projection, the continuation of the universe inside. . . . Only, to project this universe within, some outside help is needed: some kind of material, physical light, a world that is objectively new. Gardens, blue sky, or the spring. . . . Come to think of it, it's quite wrong to talk of a world within and a world without, separate worlds; there's an initial impulse of course, which starts from us, and when it can't project itself, when it can't fulfill itself objectively, when there's not total agreement between myself inside and myself outside, then it's a catastrophe, a universal contradiction, a schism.

The total agreement between self and the world is impossible: man's dreams cannot be projected into reality. So the *cité radieuse* is destroyed, like the Garden of Eden of old, by the presence of an irrational killer who is at once man's own tragic propensity toward sin and destruction—in Christian terms, man's original sin; in Freudian terms, his wishes for aggression against others and himself—and the biological fact of death. The heedless, irreparable reality of death, taken by Ionesco as by many existentialists to be the most important fact of life, indeed the singular fact of life, is confronted by Bérenger bravely in the last act of the play, but his arguments are in vain. He speaks, Ionesco notes, with "an eloquence that should underline the tragically worthless and outdated commonplaces he is advancing," refusing to strike the killer down himself though he could do so easily. Instead he resorts to sane, logical argument, appealing to the killer's supposed sense of justice, his innate sense of morality, his pragmatism, even his patriotism and altruism ("You want to destroy the world because you think it's doomed. Don't you?"), while the killer answers only with a giggle. He guesses that the killer is punishing the human race: "Perhaps you think the human race is rotten in itself. Answer me!! You want to punish the human race even in a child, the least impure of all. . . . We could debate the problem, if you like publicly, defend and oppose the motion, what do you say?" Getting no reply, he goes on to offer to the killer Christ's sacrifice:

Christ died on the Cross for *you*, it was for *you* he suffered, he *loves* you. . . . I swear to you that the blessed saints are pouring out tears for you, torrents and oceans of tears. . . . Stop sneering like that. . . . If Christ's not enough for you, I give you my solemn word I'll have an army of saviors climbing new Calvaries just for you, and have them crucified for love of you! . . .

In the end he takes out two pistols. But as the killer raises his knife, Bérenger cannot fire. He says, "Oh . . . how weak my strength is against your cold determination, your ruthlessness! And what good are bullets even, against the resistance of an infinitely stubborn will!" Man, on his knees, is helpless before the horror of his own mortality and his own mysterious, deadly self, which he cannot conquer because he cannot understand. Ionesco is able through the very ordinariness of Bérenger— the ordinariness of the man who is yet a little eloquent, "liberal," "imaginative," "intellectual"—to create in the spectator or reader the unforgettable feeling of the absurdity of life: spiritual longings in a time-locked body, a mind hopelessly divided and warring against itself.

Bérenger returns in *Rhinoceros*, slightly changed, or perhaps not the same man at all. The plot of this play is probably the most familiar of Ionesco's works: everyone in a town and by extension in the world changes into rhinoceroses. They succumb for no known reason, or because they admire the brutality of the beasts, or because they want to be like everyone else. Act 2 has what must be one of the most extraordinary scenes in theater, where a man changes into a rhinoceros onstage. His arguments are the familiar ones Ionesco speaks of as having been used by people justifying their tolerance or support of Nazism:

244

JEAN

I tell you it's not as bad as all that. After all, rhinoceroses are living creatures the same as us; they're got as much right to life as we have!

BÉRENGER

As long as they don't destroy ours in the process. You must admit the difference in mentality.

JEAN

Are you under the impression that our way of life is superior?

BÉRENGER

Well, at any rate, we have our own moral standards which I consider incompatible with the standards of these animals.

JEAN

Moral standards! I'm sick of moral standards! We need to go beyond moral standards!

BÉRENGER

What would you put in their place?

JEAN

Nature!

Even tolerance, ordinarily supposed a virtue, becomes grotesque when applied to the rhinoceroses. Another friend of Bérenger's, Dudard, argues that one must try to be rational, try to understand, that one must proceed with scientific impartiality and suppose no evil in anything that is "natural." Only experience can tell. He succumbs also, feeling that if one is going to criticize it is better to do so from the inside. The last person to leave Bérenger is his fiancée, who weakens simply because she does not want to be different from everyone else. "Perhaps it's we who need saving," she says. "Perhaps we're the abnormal ones." The animals outside are the "real people," happy to be what they are. Only man is unhappy. In a universe in which there is no absolute right, the quantitative world must become arbitrator of "right," not a single human being like Bérenger. In a final speech rather like the last soliloquy of *The Killer*, Bérenger, now alone, discovers that the rhinoceroses have somehow become beautiful and that he, the last man, has become ugly. He wishes suddenly that he could be one of them, but he cannot change; so he says, "Oh well, too bad! I'll take on the whole of them! . . . I'm the last man left, and I'm staying that way until the end. I'm not capitulating!"

To read the ending as a sound affirmation of the individual's stance against conformity or evil is surely to oversimplify Ionesco's meaning. Bérenger's last three words, "I'm not capitulating!" are noble only when taken out of the context of the speech that contains them. The satire or tragic irony is here double-edged, as it often is in Ionesco, for the brave individual is brave and individual only because, it seems, he is actually unable to be anything else. The metamorphosis of human beings into beasts is lamentable, a fact of life one takes as a brilliant metaphor for human frailty, but the final gesture of the last remaining man does not adequately oppose it. Bérenger is the "hero" here as he was the hero in *The Killer*—the most noble character of the plays' worlds, yet flawed by clichés, by blindness, by an essential hollowness as deadly in the end as the more obvious hollowness of the simpler characters who surround him. The tragic elevation of the situation is deliberately mocked; by extension, the possibilities of tragic experience seem questioned. If it is Hamlet's fate to be Hamlet, the fact that he endures his lot is perhaps tantamount to suggesting, as Freud and Ernest Jones suggest, that he is actually unable to be what he would wish; and this is the material of comedy, albeit a bitter comedy indeed. Bérenger is Ionesco's parody of the modern "tragic" individual, just as the Smiths and the Martins are parodies of parodies, or parodies of "comic" characters absolved finally of any comedy.

Shorn of specific identity and inhabiting a ghostly, barren kingdom, Bérenger returns again as the dying king in Ionesco's most recent play, *Exit the King*. Here the problem is not existence, but dying: how does one die? How does one transcend the relentless barrage of words and achieve the fact of physical death, the loss of the ego? Bérenger is an allegorical figure, a contemporary Everyman concerned not with the demands of life but with the demands of death, and the entire play is about his abandoning of the selfish, childish world of the ego (a king's kingdom) and his mystical acceptance of a mirror's reflection that does not give him back his own image. This play, while dealing with a tragic and even depressing situation, manages to be absurdly comic; Ionesco seems determined to work so precisely and relentlessly with the subject of death that he will disarm it of its power. And its structure is self-conscious, indeed: the first Queen announces flatly at the beginning of the play that the King will die "at the end of the play." This acknowledgment of artifice startles an ordinary audience, which is accustomed to the maintenance of stage verisimilitude even under the most absurd circumstances.

In Ionesco the distinctions between comedy and tragedy have been violated, reworked, discarded, lost. They are irrelevant. Comic elements occur at the most tragic moments; tragic strains undercut the comedy. The dissolving of barriers between comedy and tragedy makes possible the intensification of life at these extremes, for it is at extremes that man comes alive—or dies. Both the tragic and the comic attitudes are to Ionesco equal expressions of futility—of "absurdity," though this popular term should not be used to explain works so complex and intellectual and mysterious as Ionesco's. It is possible that, given his fragmentized view of the universe, Ionesco would be unable to deal with legitimate tragedy—in which case he would say that tragedy cannot exist, it is the highest and most stubborn of human dreams. He does not attempt to create characters, but only memorable gestures; he does not create relationships between people or their ideas, but only sharp, violent moments of collision. Clearly, such a technique is dehumanizing in that it forces our attention continually upon the abstract. Whatever humanity exists in his work is irrelevant, accidental. Does humanity exist? Ionesco's dream book, *Fragments of a Journal*, seems a recording of the resistance of a powerful mind to madness; madness is resisted, but life itself is transmuted into madness. Ionesco cries out in anguish:

What a flood of images, words, characters, symbolic figures, signs, all at the same time and meaning more or less the same thing, though never exactly the same, a chaotic jumble of messages that I may perhaps end by understanding but which tells me no more about the fundamental problem: what is this world? What is it that's all around me? Who am I? Is there an "I"? and if there is an "I" where am I going? . . . I have always been in front of a locked door. There is no key. I am waiting for the answer whereas I ought to provide it myself, to invent it. I keep waiting for a miracle that does not come. Presumably there is nothing to understand. But one's got to have a reason, to find a reason. Or else to lose one's reason.

And so Ionesco reveals himself as one of the characters in his own plays, a voice. It is not his fiction that is dehumanized, but his life. How can "humanity" exist, how can a collective sense of tragedy exist, when one cannot believe in the continuity of one's own personality? In Ionesco's plays the customary exorcising of false appearances by a heroic central character has been replaced by the confrontation of Nothing by the unwilling and poorly equipped "heroic" man. Heidegger's famous question, as it was Leibnitz's, "Why is there any being at all and not rather Nothing?" is matched by Ionesco's question, "Why is there Nothing and not, as we seem to think, as we yearn to believe, Being?" Nietzsche, in his rhapsodic praise of Heraclitus, declared that being is an empty fiction. Since it is empty, since we live in a world of becoming, we must fill it up ourselves—we must invent, we must create. But Ionesco comes closer to the gravest, most sinister truth about ourselves—being is an empty fiction, and our "becoming" is equally fictitious, equally empty, for we stand in front of locked doors, motionless, not lacking the power of motion but willed to motionlessness, waiting for a key or a miracle. There is no key, there is no miracle. Being is an empty fiction. Becoming is a nightmare from which waking is both a salvation and an annihilation.

NOTES

Notes to Chapter 1

1 Laurence Michel, "Shakespearean Tragedy: Critique of Humanism from the Inside," *Massachusetts Review*, II (1961), pp. 633–650.

2 For a wider application of Platonic ideas to *Troilus and Cressida*, see I. A. Richards, "*Troilus and Cressida* and Plato," *Hudson Review*, (1948) pp. 362–376.

3 R. A. Foakes, "*Troilus and Cressida* Reconsidered," *University of Toronto Quarterly*, XXXII (January, 1963), p. 146.

4 R. J. Kaufmann, in "Ceromonies for Chaos: The Status of *Troilus and Cressida*," *ELH*, XXXII (June 1965) sees the deep theme of the play to be the "*self-consuming* nature of all negotiable forms of vice and virtue (p. 142); the play itself is a prolegomenon to tragedy, a "taxonomical prelude to Shakespeare's mature tragedies" (p. 159). David Kaula in "Will and Reason in *Troilus and Cressida*," *Shakespeare Quarterly*, XII (1961) sees the harmony necessary between self, society, and cosmos thwarted in the play, not clearly developed as it is in the more mature tragedies (p. 283).

5 See S. L. Bethell, "*Troilus and Cressida*," in *Shakespeare: Modern Essays in Criticism*, ed. Leonard F. Dean (New York, Peter Smith, 1957), p. 265.

6 Karl Jaspers, *Reason and Existenz* (New York, 1955), p. 20.

7 See M. R. Ridley's Introduction to his edition of *Othello* in the New Arden Shakespeare (London, 1958), pp. lxvii–lxx.

8 See Wilson Knight in *Wheel of Fire* (Oxford University Press,

1935); Harold E. Toliver, "Shakespeare and the Abyss of Time," *JEGP*, LXIV (1965), pp. 243–246; and D. A. Traversi's chapter on the play in *An Approach to Shakespeare* (New York, 1956).

9 See A. S. Knowland, *"Troilus and Cressida," Shakespeare Quarterly*, X (1959), p. 359; and F. Quinland Daniels, "Order and Confusion in *Troilus and Cressida*," *Shakespeare Quarterly*, XII (1961), p. 285. Professor Knowland also questions the importance of "time" in the play.

10 George Wilbur Meyer, "Order Out of Chaos in Shakespeare's *Troilus and Cressida*," *Tulane Studies in English*, IV (1954), pp. 55–56.

11 Oscar James Campbell, *Comicall Satyre and Shakespeare's "Troilus and Cressida"* (California, 1938).

12 Foakes, *op. cit.*, pp. 146–147.

13 Achilles as the "courtly lover" obeying an oath to Polyxena not to fight is suddenly stirred to savagery when Patroclus, his "masculine whore," is killed, revealing his true love to be homosexual; Ajax, forced into a role by the cunning of Ulysses, soon swells with pride and becomes more egotistical than Achilles; Hector's change of mind has been discussed above; Pandarus seems to reveal a newer, more disgusting side of his "honey sweet" character at the end of the play.

14 See R. M. Lumiansky, "Calchas in the Early Versions of the Troilus Story," *Tulane Studies in English*, IV (1954), pp. 5–20.

15 Campbell, *op. cit.*, p. 233.

16 See Rudolf Stamm, "The Glass of Pandar's Praise: The Word Scenery, Mirror Passages, and Reported Scenes in Shakespeare's *Troilus and Cressida*," *Essays and Studies* (1964), pp. 55–77, for a detailed analysis of the self-consciousness of the play and its visual perspectives.

17 E. M. W. Tillyard, *Shakespeare's Problem Plays* (London, 1950), p. 86.

18 T. W. Baldwin, *"Troilus and Cressida Again," Scrutiny*, XVIII (1951), p. 145.

19 Hardin Craig, ed. *The Complete Works of Shakespeare* (New York, 1951), p. 863.

20 Brian Morris, "The Tragic Structure of *Troilus and Cressida*," *Shakespeare Quarterly*, X (1959), pp. 488, 491.

21 Foakes, *op. cit.*, p. 153.

22 Michel, *op. cit.*, pp. 633–650.

23 ". . . Shakespeare's ethical and intellectual world is much more agitated, multilayered, and, apart from any specific dramatic action, in itself more dramatic than that of antiquity. The very ground on which men move and actions take their course is more unsteady and

seems shaken by inner disturbances. There is no stable world as background, but a world which is perpetually re-engendering itself out of the most varied forces. . . . In antique tragedy the philosophizing is generally undramatic; it is sententious, aphoristic, is abstracted from the action and generalized, is detached from the personage and his fate. In Shakespeare's plays it becomes personal; it grows directly out of the speaker's immediate situation and remains connected with it. . . . It is dramatic self-scrutiny seeking the right mode and moment for action or doubting the possibility of finding them." Erich Auerbach, *Mimesis* (Princeton, 1953), p. 285.

Notes to Chapter 2

1 Lionel Abel, *Metatheatre* (New York, 1963), p. 50.

Notes to Chapter 3

1 Julian Hawthorne, *Nathaniel Hawthorne and His Wife: A Biography* (Boston, 1885), I, 338.
2 Richard Chase, *The American Novel and Its Tradition* (New York: Doubleday, 1957), p. 91.
3 Herman Melville, *White Jacket* (New York, 1959),. p. 269.
4 Lewis Mumford, *Herman Melville* (New York, 1929), p. 187.
5 Herman Melville, *Pierre* (New York, 1929), p. 195.
6 Leslie Fiedler, "No! in Thunder," *Esquire* (September, 1960).
7 Herman Melville, *The Confidence-Man* (Evergreen, New York, 1955), p. 133.
8 James E. Miller, Jr. "*The Confidence-Man:* His Guises," *PMLA*, LXXIV (March, 1959), p. 102–111.
9 Lawrence Thompson, *Melville's Quarrel With God* (Princeton, 1952), p. 425.
10 Walter Sutton, "Melville and the Great God Budd," *Prairie Schooner*, XXXIV (Summer 1960), p. 128–133.

Notes to Chapter 4

1 All quotes from *The Brothers Karamazov* used in this paper are taken from the Modern Library edition of the novel.
2 Sigmund Freud, "Dostoyevsky and Parricide," in the anthology *Character and Culture* (New York: Collier Books, 1963), p. 288.

3 "The Two Dimensions of Reality in *The Brothers Karamazov*," in *Creation and Discovery* (New York, 1955), pp. 55, 66.
4 *Ibid.*, p. 66.

Notes to Chapter 5

1 Quoted in David Magarshack, *Chekhov the Dramatist* (London, 1952), p. 264.
2 Quoted in Martin Esslin, *The Theater of the Absurd* (New York, 1961), p. 105.
3 Raymond Williams, "Ibsen, Miller and the Development of Liberal Tragedy," *Studies on the Left* (Spring 1964), p. 97.
4 Samuel Beckett, *Molloy* (New York, 1955), p. 33.
5 Esslin, *op. cit.*, p. 66.
6 Ezra Pound, "A Few Don'ts by an Imagist," *Poetry*, I (March 1913), p. 200–201.

Notes to Chapter 6

1 "A General Introduction for my Work," in *Essays and Introductions* (London, 1961), p. 518. Thomas Vance points out that though Dante does discourse in the third treatise of the *Convivio* about the "marvelous harmony of the body," no expression similar to "Unity of Being" occurs; the concept itself would have been meaningless to Dante, who would have held that Being had Unity by its own nature: "Being is already One." See "Dante, Yeats, and Unity of Being," *Shenandoah*, XVII, No. 2, p. 85.
2 Yeats's last play, however, *The Death of Cuchulain*, represents Cuchulain's head by means of a parallelogram, though his soul has evidently gone into the shape of a bird.
3 If the play is read as political allegory, however, the donkey is just another donkey of a nation; it is not a mysterious and sacred drama but a "satire of materialist democracy." See Donald R. Pearce, "Yeats' Last Plays: An Interpretation," *ELH*, XVIII, p. 70–71.
4 *Essays and Introductions*, p. 423.
5 Wallace Stevens, "An Ordinary Evening in New Haven."
6 Peter Ure sees the poem as embodying the "God" or force or "dramatist" of history, history being like the image of the dancer— its soul of meaning one with its body of accomplishment. See *Yeats* (Edinburgh and London, 1963), p. 117.
7 *Essays and Introductions*, p. 502.

254

Notes

8 *Ibid.*, p. 502–503.

9 It is difficult to interpret the poem as a humanistic work, imagining the poet successfully imposing his will upon the cosmos itself; see B. L. Reid, in *William Butler Yeats: The Lyric of Tragedy* (Norman, Oklahoma, 1961), p. 241. Reid sees the poet's passion stretching until it "dominates fate and creates its own world."

10 Hazard Adams speaks of Yeats's role in modern speculation about literature and art as symbolic forms: "Yeats' thought and practice lead toward the idea that there are contrary ways in which we abstract systems of reality from the flow of experience and that each of these ways offers a partial vision of reality, or presents a different *level* of reality. Yeats . . . synthesizes the neoKantian tradition of speculation about art with a Blakean dialectic." "Yeats, Dialectic and Criticism," *Criticism*, X, 3, p. 189.

11 *Essays and Introductions*, p. 421.

12 In a letter to Lady Gregory in 1902 Yeats says: "Nietzsche completes Blake and has the same roots—I have not read anything with so much excitement since I got to love Morris' stories. . . ." Yeats, *Letters*, Allan Wade, ed. (London, 1954), p. 379.

13 *Thus Spake Zarathustra*, in *The Portable Nietzsche*, translated and edited by Walter Kaufmann (New York, 1964), p. 144.

14 *Ibid.*, p. 198.

15 *Ibid.*, p. 313. Similarities exist between Nietzsche and Yeats more generally, but I have quoted from *Thus Spake Zarathustra* because Yeats refers to it frequently; he even puts himself in the role of Zarathustra, rhetorically, in the essay "Bishop Berkeley" of 1931, where he says, "If you ask me why I do not accept. . . this . . . I can but answer like Zarathustra, 'Am I a barrel of memories that I should give you my reasons?' " *Essays and Introductions*, p. 407.

16 *Essays and Introductions*, p. 243.

17 See A. G. Stock's chapter on *A Vision* in *W. B. Yeats: His Poetry and Thought* (Cambridge, England, 1961).

18 In his exhaustive study, *The Vast Design: Patterns in W. B. Yeats' Aesthetic* (Toronto, 1964), Edward Engelberg discusses Yeats's contraries in terms of expansion and contraction; he believes, however, that Yeats ultimately emerges as the "one image" in triumph over the "formless." (p. 209)

19 Critical assumption is that Yeats did, of course, desire this "Translunar paradise." See Frank Kermode, *The Romantic Image* (New York, 1957), p. 89: "[It] is precisely the concept of the dead face and the dancer, the mind moving like a top, which I am calling the central icon of Yeats and of the whole tradition. Byzantium is where this is the normal condition, where all is image and there are no con-

255

trasts and no costs, inevitable concomitants of the apparition of absolute being in the sphere of becoming."

In that milestone of Yeats criticism, *The Whole Mystery of Art: Pattern into Poetry in the Work of W. B. Yeats* (London, 1960), Giorgio Melchiori shows how the mental pattern upon which Yeats's work is built is strongly visual, approaching a geometrical scheme, and in an appendix to the book he says: "In the intuition of [a] supreme moment of fulfillment all experience is unified and rolled into one— the artist, the mystic and the sensualist share the same feeling of fullness of life and achievement . . . reaching the condition that Yeats called Unity of Being. All Yeat's life had been a pursuit of this Unity of Being, to realize at this point that it can be achieved only momentraily." (p. 285).

R. P. Blackmur sees Yeats's desire for unity as an ambition too difficult for accomplishment, which is why he is "not one of the greatest poets. . . . His curse was not that he rebelled against the mind of his age . . . but that he could not create, except in fragments, the actuality of his age, as we can see Joyce and Mann and it may be Eliot, in equal rebellion, nevertheless doing." In addition, Blackmur states that Yeats "suffered from a predominant survival in him of that primitive intellect which insists on asserting absolute order at the expense of the rational imagination." See "W. B. Yeats: Between Myth and Philosophy," in *Language as Gesture* (New York, 1953), pp. 122–123. Blackmur's assertion, of course, is highly questionable, and in this essay I hope to show something of Yeats's extreme sophistication in regard to the imposing of order upon the rational imagination.

20 *Where There Is Nothing*, in *The Variorum Edition of the Plays of W. B. Yeats* (London, Melbourne, Toronto, 1966), ed. Russell K. Alspach, p. 1158.

21 *Ibid.*, p. 688.

Yeats seems to be imposing his basically spiritual sense of reality onto Nietzsche's harsh existentialism, for, unable to believe in the Nietzschean spirituality of the body, Yeats can insist upon a mystic destruction that will free and purify the soul. Nietzsche, however, could certainly not have imagined soul without body.

22 *Plays*, p. 496.

23 See Yeats, "The Tragic Theater," in *Essays and Introductions*, pp. 240 ff.

Notes to Chapter 7

1 W. B. *Yeats and T. Sturge Moore, Their Correspondence* 1901–1937 (London, 1953), p. 156.
2 W. B. Yeats, *Essays and Introductions* (London, 1961), p. 49.
3 *Yeats at Work,* ed. Curtis B. Bradford (Carbondale, 1965), p. 215, p. 293.
4 *Essays and Introductions,* p. 279.
5 Claude Lévi-Strauss, "The Structural Study of Myth," in *Myth: A Symposium* (Bloomington, Indiana, 1965), pp. 92–3.
6 *The Variorum Edition of the Plays of W. B. Yeats,* ed. Russell K. Alspach (London, 1966), p. 963.
7 See Helen Hennessy Vendler, *Yeats' Vision and the Later Plays,* Cambridge, 1963.
8 See especially the notes to *The Only Jealousy of Emer,* in the Variorum Edition of Yeats's plays, p. 566.
9 Frank Kermode, *The Romantic Image* (New York, 1964), p. 81.
10 D. H. Lawrence, *Women in Love* (New York, 1950), p. 88.
11 *Ibid.,* p. 100.
12 W. B. Yeats, *A Vision* (New York, 1961), p. 136.
13 *Ibid.,* p. 238.
14 *Plays,* p. 574.
15 *Ibid.,* p. 807.
16 *Ibid.,* p. 569.
17 *Ibid.,* p. 574.

Notes to Chapter 8

1 In *The Portable Nietzsche,* translated and edited by Walter Kaufmann (Viking Press, 1954), p. 446.
2 *Ibid.,* p. 468.
3 Thomas Mann, *Dr. Faustus,* translated by H. T. Lowe-Porter (Modern Library, 1966), p. 243. All subsequent quotations from *Dr. Faustus* will be from this edition and the page numbers will be indicated in the text.
4 Nietzsche, *op. cit.,* p. 447.
5 Thomas Mann, *Essays of Three Decades,* translated by H. T. Lowe-Porter (New York, 1947), p. 418.
6 Dante, *The Divine Comedy,* the Carlyle-Wicksteed translation (Modern Library, 1950), p. 17.

7 Mann, *Essays*, p. 21.

8 *Ibid.*, p. 14.

9 So in *The Magic Mountain*, the snowflakes are seen as "too regular, as substance adapted to life never was to this degree—the living principle shuddered at this perfect precision, found it deathly, the very marrow of death." *The Magic Mountain*, translated by H. T. Lowe-Porter (New York, 1946), p. 480.

10 Adrian, speaking for the other side of Mann—nihilistic, aristocratic, reactionary, "barbaric"—says in a student discussion that this humanistic "radicalism" is unconvincing to him. "I cannot go along with you in your separation, after Kierkegaard, of Church and Christianity. I see the Church, even as she is today, secularized and reduced to the bourgeois, a citadel of order, an institution for objective disciplining, canalizing, banking-up of the religious life, which without her would fall victim to subjectivist demoralization, to a chaos of divine and daemonic powers, to a world of fantastic uncanniness, an ocean of daemony. To separate Church and religion means to give up separating the religious from madness" (p. 119).

11 Nietzsche, *op. cit.*, p. 44.

12 *The Magic Mountain*, p. 495.

13 Georg Lukács, *Essays on Thomas Mann*, translated by Stanley Mitchell (London, 1964), p. 97.

14 *Ibid.*, p. 88.

15 Nietzsche, *op. cit.*, p. 53.

16 Erich Kahler, "The Devil Secularized: Thomas Mann's Faust," in *Thomas Mann, A Collection of Critical Essays* (New Jersey, 1964), p. 119.

17 Horst S. Daemmrich, "Mann's Portrayal of the Artist: Archetypal Patterns," *Bucknell Review*, XIV, 3. p. 38.

18 Erich Heller, "Conversation on the Magic Mountain," in *Thomas Mann, A Collection of Critical Essays*, p. 73.

19 Hermann J. Weigand, *The Magic Mountain, A Study of Thomas Mann's "Der Zauberberg"* (Chapel Hill, 1965), p. 143.

20 Thomas Mann, *Essays*, p. 393.

21 *Ibid.*, p. 418.

22 Nietzsche, p. 549.

23 Thomas Mann, *Essays*, p. 16.

24 *Ibid.*, p. 425.

25 Steiner, *The Death of Tragedy* (New York, 1961), p. 350.

Notes to Chapter 9

1 Eugene Ionesco, "Discovering the Theatre," translated by L. C. Pronko, *Tulane Drama Review*, September, 1959.
2 Eugene Ionesco, "The Tragedy of Language," translated by Jack Undank, *Tulane Drama Review*, Spring, 1960.
3 Richard N. Coe, *Eugene Ionesco* (New York, 1961), p. 93.
4 Quoted by Martin Esselin in *The Theatre of the Absurd* (Anchor Books, 1961), p. 85.
5 Samuel Beckett, *Malone Dies* (New York, 1956), p. 52.
6 *Ibid.*, p. 77.